Easy Art Activities That
Spark Super Writing

**Mini-lessons, Quick How-to's, and Perfect Prompts That Help Kids
Learn and Apply the Elements of Great Writing**

**By Dea Paoletta Au~~
and Barbara Marica**

D1455955

SCHOLASTIC
PROFESSIONAL BOOKS

New York • Toronto • London • Auckland • Sydney
Mexico City • New Delhi • Hong Kong

Dedication

To Glenn and Marissa, the artists in my life.

—BJM

To my greatest works of art, Sam and Jack.

—DPA

Acknowledgements

Special thanks to:

Linda Hartzer for her ongoing encouragement and support. Kim Andren Hastings for her creativity, imagination, and expertise. Mary Santilli for her enthusiasm, inspiration, and flexibility. Nancy Carlin and Karli Halaby Smith for their experience, talent, and willingness to share. Glenn Mariconda for his expertise behind the lens. Our former students, especially Emily Kwong, Jessica Matis, and Casey Peterson. The student authors and artists of Mill Hill School. Our families for their love and support.

In an effort to bring this information to a wider audience, we have formed a consulting firm called Empowering Writers.
We present the ideas in this book at workshops and seminars for educators.
For information on workshops and seminars, call (203) 374-8125 or write:
Empowering Writers, P.O. Box 4, Easton, CT 06612
or see us on the Web at www.empoweringwriters.com

Front cover design by Norma Ortiz
Interior design by Melinda Belter
Illustration on page 60 by Cary Pillo
Photos on pages 8 and 18 by Kalman and Pabst Photo Group
Photo on page 66 by Joan Beard
All others courtesy of authors

ISBN 0-439-16518-0
Copyright 2000 by Dea Paoletta Auray and Barbara Mariconda, all rights reserved

Table of Contents

Introduction
The Power of the Art Connection 4

1. Story Summaries
The key to understanding a story's basic parts 8
WRITER'S TECHNIQUE: Identifying the main elements of a story
    CINDERELLA (before-and-after diamond foldouts, pyramid foldies) 9

2. Elaborative Detail
The sights, sounds, tastes, and smells that make stories come alive 13
WRITER'S TECHNIQUE: Describing a setting
    AUTUMN SCENE (crayon, watercolor wash) 16
    MOUSE IN MEADOW (torn paper) 20
    DREAM ROOM (collage) 24

WRITER'S TECHNIQUE: Describing a character
    SNOWMAN (sponge-painting with 3-D details) 28
    FRIENDLY SCARECROW (cut paper with natural touches) 32
    PIRATE (cut-and-pasted pirates) 36

WRITER'S TECHNIQUE: Describing an object/animal
    JUNGLE CREATURE (tissue-paper collage) 40
    GINGERBREAD HOUSE (cardboard/candy mosaics) 44
    ANCIENT CROWN (decorated oaktag crowns) 48

3. Suspense
Using word referents and the Magic of Three pattern to build dramatic tension . . 52
WRITER'S TECHNIQUE: Building suspense
    WHO'S INSIDE THE MITTEN? (construction-paper mitten with drawing) 54
    WHO'S GOBBLING? (plastic-cup turkey) 58
    WHO'S HAUNTING THIS HOUSE? (haunted house cutout, lift-the-flap activity) 62

4. Main Event
Every story needs a central action around which the characters turn 66
WRITER'S TECHNIQUE: Creating a fully elaborated main event
    LEPRECHAUN CHASE (leprechaun spinners) 68
    MAGIC CARPET RIDE (a woven carpet) 72
    OUCH! (Band-Aid™ picture) 76

Resources 80

Introduction

The Power of the Art Connection

You've heard the cliché *a picture paints a thousand words.* The photo and writing sample below demonstrate that a picture not only paints a thousand words but also inspires words—words that are descriptive, evocative, and convincing. For children, this art/writing connection is particularly powerful, especially when the artwork is their own creation. The activities in this book are designed to nurture the symbiotic connections between art and writing in a number of ways:

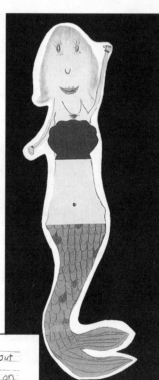

1. To use art as a **concrete visual resource** for students to reference as they write (through depictions of colorful scenes, expressive characters, and fascinating objects)

2. To use art as a **means of inspiring and translating** the power of specific visual detail into vivid writing, improving word choice and vocabulary

3. To use art as a **creative, fun means** of managing the process-writing classroom

4. To use art as a **way to motivate and inspire** students for whom writing is difficult

STUDENT SAMPLE

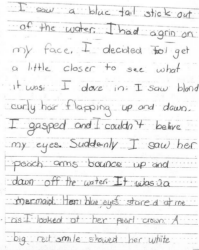

I saw a blue tail stick out of the water. I had a grin on my face. I decided I get a little closer to see what it was. I dove in. I saw blond curly hair flapping up and down. I gasped and I couldn't belive my eyes. Suddenly I saw her peach arms bounce up and down off the water. It was a mermaid. Her blue eyes stared at me as I looked at her pearl crown. A big red smile showed her white clean teeth.

Using Art to Get Kids Writing

This fourth benefit—art as a way to motivate and inspire students—is perhaps the most compelling. For many students, getting started on a piece of writing is the hardest part. However, if students first create pictures or a model that relates to their theme or topic, they can use this concrete object as their starting point. It's much easier for students to write about the characteristics of a character, setting, or event as depicted in their artwork than it is to visualize these details in the abstract. Using art as a springboard into the creative process helps students to better express themselves in writing.

For example, let's say you've just finished reading your students a series of tall tales and have decided that you'd like them to create and describe a tall-tale character of their own, perhaps a "Timberland Tom" or a "Mountain Marie" to join Paul Bunyan and others you've read about. How much easier (and more fun!) it is to begin by having students draw their huge characters on

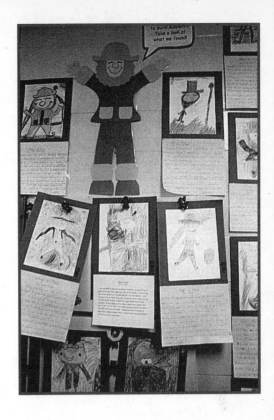

large pieces of construction paper, using paint, crayons, scraps of cloth, buttons, and yarn to complete their characters' rugged features and outdoorsy garb. Students begin to see their characters in specific terms and can be held accountable for including these specific details in their writing. You can make the written portion of an activity such as this even more fun by displaying collections of artwork on one side of a bulletin board and the written descriptions on the opposite side. Then challenge students to match the artistic rendering to the corresponding written description. This gives students even more incentive to include as many specific details as possible!

The Benefits to Classroom Management

Having an art component for a writing activity helps in the management of the writer's workshop. If a writing project has a companion art component, students are always working on some portion of their assignment—the art connection or the actual writing. Rather than waiting idly for conferences, students can work on a related art project that deepens their understanding of writers' techniques, such as generating vivid, specific details or focusing on a significant event. This frees you to conference with individual students or to deliver a mini-lesson to a small group while the rest of the class is working productively.

Incorporating art into your classroom is a terrific way to facilitate flexible grouping in writing. First, assess the needs of the writers in your class. Present a whole-class lesson on a particular skill. Then, set your more able writers to work independently on the art connection while you meet with your needier writers to reteach and reinforce the particular skill, modeling it for them again. As these students proceed with the art project, you are free to conference with your more able writers as they move to translate their artistic vision into writing.

Integrating Art Activities Into the Curriculum

The art activities in this book are easily adaptable to specific themes or units that you teach. For example, if you're studying the rain forest, you can modify any of the art projects designed to describe an outdoor setting to depict the rain forest (for instance, the *Autumn Scene* might become a *Jungle View*). In this way, these activities can be a terrific vehicle for writing across the curriculum—integrating your writer's workshop, language arts, social studies, and science programs.

We have also provided you with a list of books that relate thematically to each art/writing project. Gather some of these from your school library as you begin each activity. Students will move from the books to their art to their writing, and back again, each component enriching and strengthening the others—all of which will translate into better writing!

Bringing Art Into Your Writing Workshop

The activities in the following sections have been designed to help you easily integrate art into your writing lessons. The basic format follows.

1. Introduce the writing skill (we refer to it as the Writer's Technique).

2. Model the writing skill, working from the student page.

3. Invite students to create their own art and then write about it; the art activity inspires and focuses the guided practice.

You may vary the way you incorporate the art component of the lesson, depending on your students' needs and the particular project. An overview of each lesson component is provided below.

INTRODUCE THE WRITING SKILL

WRITER'S TECHNIQUE Use the introductory page(s) at the beginning of each section—*Story Summaries, Elaborative Detail, Suspense,* and *Main Event*—to define and introduce the particular skill to students. Try using your own or student work, a piece of literature, or perhaps a movie all are familiar with to show how a particular writing skill can be used to engage the reader.

MODEL THE WRITING SKILL

Once you've introduced the skill, choose an activity (there are multiple activities for each writing technique) and model the writing skill for students. Using the prompts from the student page, ask students to help you brainstorm ideas and record them on chart paper or an overhead transparency. Then use the teacher page(s) to walk students through the writing activity, "thinking aloud" about how you transform your brainstormed ideas into complete sentences that make up a paragraph. In this way you demonstrate the thought processes of an author. We have found that this is the most effective teaching tool you can use, a strategy that produces powerful results but is often overlooked in the instruction of writing. There is sometimes an assumption that if students are exposed to high-quality, published pieces of writing, and if they discuss the characteristics of that writing that make it effective, they will then be able to incorporate similar elements into their own writing. This is a stretch for most students.

Here's an analogy to illustrate this point: Imagine going to a restaurant and enjoying a fine meal. You could identify many of the ingredients and perhaps even the method of cooking. Yet, even after experiencing and analyzing the meal, would you be able to go home and produce a similar dish? Most people could not. However, if the chef walked you through the cooking process step by step (modeled it), you would have a much better chance of producing the fine meal! It is the same with writing. By demonstrating the process step by step, you give your students a clear sense of what it takes to apply the particular skill to their own writing.

GUIDED PRACTICE

In guided practice, students work through the same writing activity you modeled for them, guided by the prompts and sentence starters on the student page, your written examples that remain posted in the room, their artwork, and, of course, you. After you've modeled the specific writing skill and (in most cases) students have completed the art activity, distribute the writing activity sheet to students and invite them to practice the writing skill. They can consult your example and their artwork for ideas and for help in generating specific detail and staying focused on their topic. Practicing the skill in isolation gives students the experience they need to then apply the skill in their own work.

You may be concerned that students will merely copy your example. Not to worry: They won't copy word for word—rather, they will use your example as a guide. Consider this example of guided practice from math.

Think about teaching a tricky math skill, say, regrouping in subtraction. Think of the way you model many examples. You talk students through them, write out the numbers, illustrate groups of tens and ones, demonstrate the specific "borrowing" procedure. Then, of course, you leave this posted as you set them to the task of subtracting and regrouping on their own. Students will proceed with their work, constantly referencing your example. They will do the same with writing, adding their own creative ideas and individual preferences.

Circulate through the classroom as students write, offering assistance, encouragement, and praise. Share excellent examples aloud. Students can learn as much from their peers as they do from you!

Story Summaries

Summarizing a story is a critical skill for the young author. Summarizing involves recognizing a story's structure and reducing it to its most basic elements. If young students summarize each narrative story they read, they eventually assimilate the underlying story patterns. This comprehension activity is also a prewriting skill that enables children to formulate story plans successfully.

When summarizing a story, students need to identify more than the beginning, middle, and end. By discovering how the main character has changed as a result of the story events, students begin to see how the author develops character. In other words, what was the main character's struggle or challenge? What did the main character want? What was the main character's motivation? At the story's conclusion, how is the main character different than he/she was at the beginning of the story? What has he/she learned or decided as a result? Which character traits affected the manner in which the main character dealt with and solved his/her problem? An awareness of these critical questions brings student readers and writers to a deeper level of understanding story, which, over time, will translate into their own writing.

The following summarizing activities (pages 9–12) using diamond foldouts and pyramid foldies help students sequence story events and highlight the growth or changes that the main character experienced. These art activities can be adapted to almost any narrative story your students read!

Cinderella

 **Identifying the main elements of a story.**

INTRODUCE

Ask students how many have heard the story of Cinderella (or Jack in the Beanstalk or another familiar tale). Ask a volunteer to retell the story for the class, focusing on the key points. Once the student finishes the retelling, ask the class how it was different from the full story, drawing out the differences between a summary and a fully elaborated story.

Next, obtain a copy of *Cinderella* (or whatever story you choose) from your school library and read it aloud to your class. (Choose a version with lots of elaborative detail.) After reading it, point out the elaborative details, suspense, and fully elaborated events, techniques students will practice later in the school year.

LITERATURE CONNECTION

The Golden Sandal
by Rebecca Hickox

Egyptian Cinderella **by Shirley Climo**

Irish Cinderlad **by Shirley Climo**

Bigfoot Cinderella
by Mike Thaler

MODEL

As a class, answer the questions on the *Cinderella* student page (p. 12), which ask students to identify the beginning, middle, and end of the story and to think about the main character's growth or change. (You may want to make an overhead transparency of the page and lead the students through each question.) Answering these questions helps lay the groundwork for prewriting by emphasizing the key characteristics of story—character, problem, motivation, struggle, solution or conclusion—and the ways in which the events of the story shape and change character. Similar questions may be applied to any narrative story for the purposes of story planning and comprehension.

ART CONNECTION

Before-and-After Diamond Foldouts

MATERIALS
• 10" x 10" squares of construction paper
• crayons, markers

PROCEDURE

1. Distribute construction paper to students. Demonstrate how to fold squares in half diagonally, forming a triangle by matching corners. Then fold the resulting triangle in half again, producing a smaller triangle. See Step 1; the dotted lines represent the folds.

2. Unfold paper as shown in Step 1 and then refold each corner point in toward the center where original folds intersect, as shown in Step 2. (This will result in a square shape; see Step 3.)

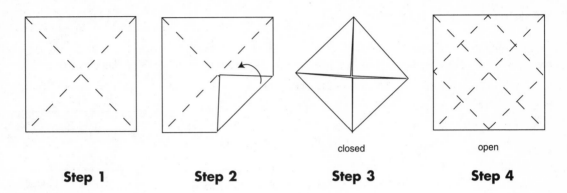

closed   open

Step 1   **Step 2**   **Step 3**   **Step 4**

3. Crease folds deeply so that triangular flaps stay flat. Ask students to draw Cinderella at the beginning of the story right over the triangular flaps. (This will require them to hold the flaps in place.) Draw her as large as the paper will allow. Encourage them to add as many details as they can—ragged clothing, soot and dirt, her broom and bucket, the sad expression on her face. This is the "Before" picture.

4. Next, unfold each triangle as shown in Step 4, and within the inner square revealed, draw the "After" version of Cinderella. Encourage students to draw her in about the same size and relative position as the "Before" version. The only difference will be in the details—her finery and her happy expression.

Cinderella–before

Cinderella–after

ALTERNATIVE ART ACTIVITY

Pyramid Foldies

This is another art activity that helps students visualize story structure and practice summarizing. It, too, works with any familiar tale, and you can use the same reproducible student page (p. 12). The foldies on this page were created for *Jack and the Beanstalk.*

MATERIALS
- 10" x 10" squares of construction paper
- crayons, markers
- glue, tape, or staples

PROCEDURE

1. Distribute paper to students. Demonstrate how to fold squares in half diagonally into a triangle, matching corners; see Step 1. Then fold the resulting triangle in half again, producing a smaller triangle as shown in Step 2. Unfold the paper and lightly label the four corners A, B, C, and D; label the center point, where the folds intersect, as E. (See Step 3.)

2. Cut along one fold from point C to midpoint E as shown in Step 3.

3. Slide the left-hand, newly cut C corner over to point D. This step creates a 3-D figure, as illustrated in Step 4. Explain that students will use a triangle to depict the beginning, middle, and end of their story. They can lay their papers flat while they illustrate, keeping in mind the position of each triangle in the 3-D figure.

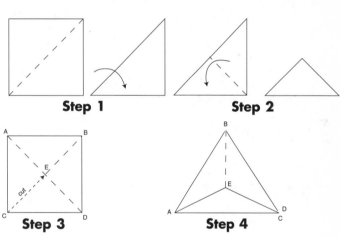

Step 1 **Step 2**

Step 3 **Step 4**

4. After students draw and color a picture representing the beginning, middle, and end in each triangle, slide the C corner back over to point D and glue in place. The foldy should stand up, as pictured in the photograph.

GUIDED PRACTICE

Hand out the *Cinderella* student page and encourage students to answer the questions in their own words, referring to their foldouts or foldies and using the class model as an example. Students can practice summarizing in small groups, using their artwork to prompt their retelling.

Name _____ Date _____

IMAGINE THAT . . .

At the beginning of *Cinderella,* we find poor Cinderella dressed in rags and covered in soot. She carries a bucket in one hand and a broom in the other.

In the end, we see Cinderella again, this time dressed in satin and lace, with a crown upon her head, her lovely hair set in curls and waves, sparkling glass slippers on her feet. She has been transformed!

ASK YOURSELF . . .

In the beginning . . .

- What was Cinderella's problem at the beginning of the story? _____
  _____

- What did Cinderella want more than anything else? _____
  _____

In the middle . . .

- How did Cinderella get her wish? _____
  _____

- What was her challenge after her wish was granted? _____
  _____

In the end . . .

- How was Cinderella's problem solved? _____
  _____

- How is her life different than it was in the beginning of the story? _____
  _____

These are questions that the author asked while planning the story. In most stories, the author begins with a character who has a problem or who wants something and sets out to solve the problem or accomplish a goal of some kind. The middle of a story shows how the main character struggles and works toward solving the problem. At the end of a story, we see how the problem was solved and how the main character has changed. You can use this story pattern to help plan your own stories!

Elaborative Detail

Elaborative detail breathes life into a narrative and allows the reader to experience the story right along with the main character. When an author writes an elaborative segment within a narrative, he or she stops the action to paint a picture of a story-critical setting, character, or object with sensory detail.

IDENTIFYING STORY-CRITICAL ELEMENTS

How can you help your students determine a story-critical character, setting, or object? We ask our students to imagine a photograph of characters, settings, or objects that are important to their stories. Author and educator Barry Lane refers to this technique as a "snapshot." In writing, just as in photography, we don't take random pictures. We reserve film (or blocks of description) for only truly memorable people, places, and things. In our classrooms we've practiced identifying story-critical characters, settings, and objects through a questioning game of "What if?"

To begin, we pose the question, "What if I were writing a story about a giant chasing me through the mountains?" Then, we think aloud for students about how that story might develop. Finally, we ask students, "What character would be critical to our story? What part would you want to 'photograph' with words?" Students respond with the images they'd like to see—the giant, the scary mountains—which turn out to be the story-critical character and setting. There's no end to the "What if?" game—"What if you met a Sand Monster in the desert driving a magic dune buggy?" "What if you opened the refrigerator and the celery started talking to you?" Playing this game helps students generate story ideas and identify story-critical elements.

USING ELABORATIVE DETAIL TO "SHOW," NOT "TELL"

Once students can identify story-critical characters, settings, and objects, they learn how to stop the story action and describe these important elements. This technique is referred to in many ways; the body of literature on the craft of writing uses the terminology "show, don't tell."

Take a look at this sentence:

There stood an awesome scarecrow.

Here the writer simply tells us what she sees. Now read this:

I stared at the scarecrow, who stood as tall as the tallest cornstalk in the field! A pair of ragged denim overalls hugged his skinny body. A red plaid shirt covered his long arms and narrow chest. A pair of old, dirty work gloves hung from his sleeves and flapped about in the breeze. I could barely take my eyes off the wide straw hat that perched on his head. Straggly corn-silk hair hung beneath the hat. I smiled as I gazed into his merry, red-radish eyes and dried-up corncob nose. His head was a huge, round pumpkin with a wide, toothless grin carved out. He seemed to be stuffed with hay, which sprouted out here and there. He held a large rake in his hands.

What a difference! Notice how the scarecrow is brought to life through the use of specific rather than general adjectives and verbs. It is not a "grocery list" of details: "The scarecrow wore denim overalls, a plaid shirt, work gloves, and a straw hat"; rather, it is a series of sentences with specific detail in each. These small brushstrokes of specificity can improve a piece of writing.

It is not only physical description that brings a story to life. An important part of plot—the ways in which a main character approaches the story problem—depends on character traits and mood. In vivid storytelling, character traits, personality, and mood are also *shown* rather than *told*. In other words, description and specific detail can be used to reveal character! Let's look at an example:

Jack was worried.

That would be *telling*. Here's how an author can use elaborative detail to *show* the same thing:

Jack wrung his hands and shook his head. He stared off into the distance, nibbled his bottom lip, and frowned.

Allowing the audience to see and experience Jack's worry is much more effective than simply telling them that he is worried!

Here is another example:

The old cat was mean.

That would be *telling*. Look at how a writer could use elaborative detail to *show* the same thing:

The old cat slunk forward with her back arched in the air. She stared through yellow eyes narrowed into two slits. She hissed at me and pulled back her mouth, revealing a row of sharp, white, pointy teeth.

So, how can we help children write descriptive segments within their narrative stories that bring their story-critical characters, settings, and objects to life? See below for a step-by-step procedure that moves writing from general *telling* to specific *showing*.

GENERATING ELABORATIVE DETAIL

1. Remind students that authors use elaborative detail when they want to focus on a story-critical setting, character, or object. Give examples of this. For instance, if the story is about exploring an abandoned house, the story-critical setting would be the house. The story-critical character or object may be someone or something the main character discovers in the house.

2. Generate questions about the topic around relevant attributes and characteristics, such as color, shape, size, material, weight, age, texture, condition, facial features, physical characteristics, mood, temperament, sound, smell. (Facial features and body posture are the best indicators of mood and character traits.) Encourage students to use sensory detail, reminding them to include sound, feel, taste, and smell in addition to sight.

3. Brainstorm with the class and list ideas on chart paper. (Examples of this technique are annotated in each elaborative detail activity.)

4. Model transforming the list of ideas into complete sentences and then creating a paragraph. No grocery lists or redundant sentence structures allowed!

5. Encourage students to continue independently. Circulate and compliment them as they work. Read good illustrative examples aloud.

   The nine activities in the following section guide students through describing settings, characters, and objects with elaborative detail.

Autumn Scene

WRITER'S TECHNIQUE ▷ Describe a setting.

INTRODUCE

Introduce elaborative detail to the class, emphasizing sensory detail. Try tying this writing technique to a topic your students are currently studying. For example, if you're studying habitats, point out that students can use this skill to describe their chosen habitats in their science reports.

LITERATURE CONNECTION

Autumn, an Alphabet Acrostic by Steven Schnur

Autumn Leaves by Ken Robbins

How Do You Know It's Fall? by Allan Fowler

MODEL

Model how you ask yourself questions about an outdoor scene in order to conjure the sensory details you need to write a description that captures the scene in writing, and encourage students to jump in and contribute ideas. Prepare a chart on which to record your and the class's responses; see the graphic organizer bellow for an example. Think aloud about your autumn scene, asking yourself what autumn looks like, smells like, feels like, tastes like, and sounds like. It's helpful to have a picture (or pictures!) of an autumn scene to help inspire you and your students; see the literature connections box above for ideas. Your chart might look something like this:

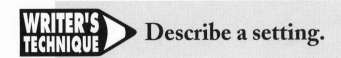

What does autumn . . .

Look like?
leaves changing colors, pumpkins and jack-o'-lanterns, people raking leaves, cornstalks, Indian corn, scarecrows perched on porches, squirrels gathering nuts

Feel like?
cool breezes, chilly nights, leaves crunching underfoot

Smell like?
burning leaves, crisp cool air, a nearby fire, pumpkin pies baking, freshly made apple cider, cinnamon

Sound like?
trick-or-treaters knocking on the door, wind rustling dry leaves, crackling fires, kids playing soccer, people raking leaves

Taste like?
apple cider, apple pie, pumpkin pie

Once you have charted all the suggestions from the class, model writing a paragraph that incorporates a selection of details into a vividly drawn autumn scene. Use sentence starters from the *Autumn Scene* student page (p.19) and think aloud about your choices as you write.

It was a beautiful autumn day. As I looked around, I noticed that leaves were beginning to change into the fiery reds and oranges of the season. I could see the animals scurrying about gathering nuts, preparing for the cold winter days that loomed ahead. The cool breeze scattered the leaves in all directions and sent a chill down my spine. I took a deep breath and was warmed instantly by the smell of a nearby fire. My mouth began to water as I thought about the taste of a freshly baked hot apple pie.

ART CONNECTION

MATERIALS
- oaktag
- scissors
- scrap paper for covering desks
- watercolor paints in autumn colors (orange, yellow, red, brown)
- small containers of water for diluting color
- large watercolor brushes

PREPARATION
Prepare leaves by cutting them out of oaktag; you'll need one for each student. Alternatively, you can have students draw and cut out their own leaves, either from a template or freehand.

PROCEDURE
1. Distribute an oaktag leaf to each student (or have them cut their own) along with scrap paper to cover the desks.

2. Hand out the watercolors, brushes, and clean water. Discuss the colors of autumn and let students choose colors they feel are appropriate for autumn leaves. Give students time to practice watering down colors on scrap paper.

3. Once they are used to using the watercolors and diluting colors, invite them to paint their leaves in a blended combination of autumn colors.

4. Set the leaves aside to dry. Then have students arrange them around the class tree on a bulletin board. Finally, add their descriptions of the autumn scene.

STUDENT SAMPLE

To me, autumn looks like brown, red, and yellow leaves falling to the forest floor. I heard the sound of fire in the fireplace . . . crackle, crackle, crackle. When I breathed in, I noticed the smell of spicy apple cider.
I can just imagine the salty taste of crispy pumpkin seeds. When I touched the big, plump pumpkin, it felt bumpy on its skin.

There were bright orange pumpkins growing in a patch. I noticed geese flying in the air making noise. Honk, honk, honk went the wild geese. "Mmmmm." I smelled Halloween candy—Snickers and Kit cats! The leaves felt crunchy and dry beneath my feet. My mouth waters when I think of juicy apple pie!

I watched squirrels gathering nuts and noticed chipmunks running here and there. To me, autumn sounds like people raking leaves of all colors. Ch, ch, ch went the rake. When I went outside, I smelled candy apples and cotton candy at the autumn fair. I can just imagine the sweet taste of candy on Halloween. I love the feeling of autumn wind in my hair.

GUIDED PRACTICE

Leaving all the practice charts posted, distribute the Autumn Scene student page and invite students to write their own description of an autumn day. Encourage them to use their own ideas and remind them to use sentence variety.

Name _____ Date _____

IMAGINE THAT . . .

You are outside on a beautiful autumn day. You look around and take a deep breath. Describe the autumn day using all your senses.

Writer's Technique   Describing a setting.

Artful Connection   Create an autumn tree for the classroom.

Get Ready to Write!   This activity asks you to use *all* your senses. Think about what autumn

looks like • feels like • tastes like • smells like • sounds like

On another piece of paper, brainstorm your ideas, trying for at least two details for each sense. Then choose at least one detail for each sense, and write about it in a complete sentence. The sentence starters below can help you get going.

Sight

As I looked around, I noticed . . .

I could see . . .

Glancing around me, I saw . . .

I gazed at . . .

Sound

Standing quietly, I noticed . . .

As I listened . . .

In the distance, I could hear . . .

I strained to hear . . .

Smell

I took a deep breath and . . .

I noticed the smell of . . .

In the far-off distance, I could smell . . .

Touch

I could feel . . .

When I ran my hand along it, it . . .

As I touched it, I realized . . .

. . . felt like

Taste

I could taste . . .

My mouth watered as I thought . . .

Remembering the taste of . . .

I licked my lips just thinking about . . .

Mouse in Meadow

 **WRITER'S TECHNIQUE** ▷ Describing a setting.

INTRODUCE

Introduce elaborative detail to students, reminding them of the importance of sensory details. For a fun twist, ask students to pretend they are mice and to think about what sights, sounds, tastes, and smells a mouse would notice in a meadow!

LITERATURE CONNECTION

Frederick by Leo Lionni
This book uses the same torn-paper technique presented here.

MODEL

Model how you can use the questions on the *Mouse in Meadow* student page (p.23) to generate ideas for your descriptive paragraph, asking students for their contributions. It is helpful if you have a picture of a meadow or other spring scene to set the mood. Chart as many of the student responses as you can. Your chart may look like this:

What did the mouse look like?

small
gray
long tail
pink nose
brown
whiskered face

What kind of growing things are found in the meadow?

tall, green grass
dandelions
daffodils
violets
puffy bushes
flowering trees

What kind of wildlife did the mouse find?

a lone deer
a small bunny
birds flying back and forth
   to their nest
butterflies
grasshoppers
dragonflies

What sounds would the mouse hear?

birds chirping
wind rustling the grass
leaves swishing
bees buzzing
squirrels chattering

What might the mouse smell?

flowers
honeysuckle
green grass
clean, crisp air

What would the mouse feel?

a cool breeze
warm sunlight
soft grass
mushy mud

Choose the details that you would like to include in your description. Think aloud for students as you transform them on the chart paper into complete sentences, making a paragraph that might look like this:

The gray mouse lifted his head toward the clear, blue sky. He wiggled his whiskered nose and sniffed. Ahhh, there was nothing like the meadow in springtime. Sweet-smelling daffodils and violets swayed in a soft breeze. He scampered through the tall, green grass and played tag with a cheerful butterfly. Bees buzzed lazily from flower to flower as a deer and her fawn tiptoed nearby. The mouse stretched out in the grass and enjoyed the warmth of the sun on his tiny back.

ART CONNECTION

MATERIALS
- scraps of construction paper in assorted colors
- crayons
- white construction paper
- glue, tape
- fine-line black markers

PROCEDURE

1. Gather students around and invite them to create a meadow scene using torn paper. Show them how to tear paper into shapes that will make up the objects in their scene.

2. Demonstrate how to create the mouse by holding a piece of gray or brown paper closely between your thumb and forefinger. Then gently tear the paper with your other thumb and forefinger, slowly and carefully making an oval shape that's at least two inches across. You can also tear small ears and legs out of contrasting color, and you may want to further demonstrate how to tear grass, flowers, or other meadow inhabitants.

3. Distribute the crayons and colored paper and encourage kids to design their own meadow scene on a background of white construction paper.

4. Next, explain that they will be using crayons to fill in the meadow background—the ground, the sky, or any details that are too small or complicated to tear, such as small flowers or insects.

5. Once finished with their backgrounds, students will glue down their torn-paper mice and add details (whiskers, tails, eyes, nose, mouth) with a fine-line black marker.

6. Students can add additional torn paper or crayon details to their pictures.

GUIDED PRACTICE

Leaving all the practice charts posted, ask students to write their own description of a mouse in the meadow. Encourage them to use their own ideas and remind them to use sentence variety. They may even want to name the mouse! As they work, circulate around the room offering guidance and asking questions to help students generate their descriptions.

STUDENT SAMPLE

Hayley   #03 March 3 2000

Sniff! Sniff! went Frederick's soft pink nose as he smelled the fraggrant flowers that looked like they had jelly filling. He noticed the grass was flaky and was coverd with dew. The next thing he knew, he could smell the rich, golden honey sourrounding him. Suddenly Frederick heard the sweet songs of birds chirping. Befor he knew I, he saw blueberrys on a puffy green bush. Suddenly, Frederick yawned. Slowly he went back to his little house and fell sound asleep.

SIZZLING

Mouse in Meadow Student Page

Name _____ Date _____

IMAGINE THAT . . .

A small, gray mouse enjoys a lovely meadow on a beautiful spring day!

Writer's Technique Describing a setting.

Artful Connection Create a mouse and meadow scene with crayon and torn paper.

Get Ready to Write! Think about springtime in a meadow, using your torn-paper scene for inspiration. Next, answer these five questions. Jot down anything that pops into your mind. This will give you terrific details about the mouse in the meadow.

1. What did the mouse look like? _____

2. What kinds of things grow in the meadow? _____

3. What kind of wildlife did the mouse find? _____

4. What sounds would the mouse hear? _____

5. What might the mouse smell? _____

On another piece of paper, turn your ideas into complete sentences. These sentence starters may help you. You may want to give your mouse a name.

The small creature had . . .

The mouse . . .

As the mouse looked around, . . .

Standing quietly, he/she noticed . . .

To Mouse's surprise, he/she saw. . .

Just then, Mouse could see . . .

Off in the distance, . . .

When Mouse touched it, . . .

Mouse took a deep breath and . . .

The smell reminded him/her of . . .

Listening carefully, . . .

Dream Room

 **WRITER'S TECHNIQUE** ▶ Describing a setting.

INTRODUCE

Introduce elaborative detail, building on previous lessons. When you ask students to imagine their dream room, remind them that the sky's the limit! Encourage them to let their imaginations go and not be bound by reality.

LITERATURE CONNECTION

A Place for Ben
by Jeanne Titherington

Clean Your Room, Harvey Moon!
by Pat Cummings

MODEL

Working from the questions on the *Dream Room* student page (p.27), invite your students to help you generate lots of details about a dream room. Having a picture or collage to focus your think-aloud is a great help. Encourage students to not only describe your picture but also to gather ideas for their own room. Your charted responses might look like this:

My Dream Room . . .

Color
lime green
pale pink
cobalt blue
rainbow colors

Furniture
cozy, overstuffed chairs
a bunk bed with a fort
    underneath
huge, fluffy pillows
a game table

Windows
large window with a seat
tall windows going from
    floor to ceiling
porthole windows

Floor
carpet squares connecting
    together
long, white, furry rug
multicolored tiles
brick
game boards painted
    on the floor

Ceiling
chandelier
mobiles
stars
moon
sun and clouds
birds
glass disco ball
swing

Decorations
fish tank
lava lamp
posters
paintings
cuckoo clock
juke box
pinball machine

Sounds
fish tank gurgling
beeping sounds of
    the pinball machine
the stereo playing

Select an assortment of details and use them to create a descriptive paragraph for your dream room. Think aloud as you compose on chart paper. Your paragraph might look something like this:

My room is awesome! From floor to ceiling, the room is cobalt blue. The dark-blue ceiling is the perfect backdrop for my glow-in-the-dark moon and stars that shine over me as I sleep. In the daytime, a large mirrored ball spins from the center of the ceiling, capturing the sunlight and sending it sparkling back in a million fragments. From my cozy bed of over-stuffed pillows, I can see my fish tank full of tropical fish surprises, and at night when I am very quiet its gurgling sound lulls me to sleep. When I don't feel like sleeping, there is plenty to do! I just look down. My bedroom floor is a giant game board! Checkers, chess, backgammon, you name it, I can play it. When a good book will do, I just plop down in one of my overstuffed chairs, put my feet up, and read to my heart's content.

ART CONNECTION

MATERIALS
- white or manila 9" x 12" construction paper (1 piece for each student)
- crayons
- many magazines and catalogs, especially those with a home-decorating theme
- scissors
- glue sticks

PROCEDURE

1. Distribute the paper to the students. Using the crayon color of their choice, they can "paint" the walls of their dream room.

2. Allow plenty of time for students to peruse the magazines and choose the furniture, decorations, rug or carpet, window dressings, knickknacks, and other neat stuff they would include in their dream room. Remind them that the room will be far more interesting if they include lots of small details, and discourage them from cutting out an already decorated room from the magazine. (This step could also be done as part of a homework activity.)

3. Students then "lay out" their rooms and glue down the picture once they're satisfied with their design. Since their picture is not three-dimensional, they will need to determine the floor line by drawing a horizontal line across the paper. The bottom half of the paper will be the floor and the top half the wall.

Display Idea

When the rooms dry, you can make a bulletin board by connecting and stacking all the rooms together. Add a construction-paper roof and you have a classroom dream house!

GUIDED PRACTICE

Working from their completed collage, students can brainstorm the details of their dream room and then compose a descriptive paragraph. Remind them to use the sentence starters on the student page for sentence variety.

STUDENT SAMPLE

Lily   #14 March.10, 2000   aSmith

My room is SUPER! The clean floor is carnation Pink. As I look around my room I notice the sky blue walls are painted beautifully. A butterfly clock ticking loudly told me it was 3:24. I also see my green fluffy bed I have slept in for years. It is very special to me. Along with it came seven soft pillows in different shapes and sizes. A huge piece of watermelon sits on a plate on the little table next to my bed because I LOVE watermelon. Many white flowers with green stems are sitting behind the piece of watermelon. Listening carefully

LOVE watermelon. Many white flowers with green stems are sitting behind the piece of watermelon. Listening carefully I hear my rocking chair rock slowly back and forth. My soccer ball sits steadily behind my drawers for my clothes. One big teddy bear sits on the bed, and the smaller bear sits on the larger bear. I stare at the green shoe holder with seven pairs of shoes placed in separate slots. They look like they are waiting to be used. "BRING!" went the clock. "It's exactly 4:00!" "Whatever!" I thought. Four Dr. Seuss books are stacked on top of each other. "I love my room!" I say to myself.

Dream Room Student Page

Name _____ Date _____

IMAGINE THAT . . .

▪▪▪

You can design the room of your dreams.

Writer's Technique   Describing a setting.

Artful Connection   Cut out pictures from magazines that have details you'd like to include in your dream room. Some things to look for might include furniture, carpeting, windows, curtains, lamps, and any items that you particularly like. Then, "paint" the room using crayons. Remember to choose your dream color! Finally, glue down all the details of your room.

Get Ready to Write!   Look at the dream room you have created. Then answer these questions to help you come up with terrific details about your room.

What color is your room? _____

What kind of furniture is in your room? _____

What kind of windows are in the room? _____

What is the floor like? _____

What is hanging from the ceiling? _____

What items decorate the room? _____

What sounds are unique to your room? _____

On another paper, turn your ideas into complete sentences, and create a paragraph describing your wonderful room. These sentence starters may help you!

As I looked around my room, . . .   Tucked in the corner was . . .

This place is special because . . .   You would be surprised by . . .

I could not help but enjoy . . .   It reminded me of . . .

I stared at my . . .   Listening carefully, I noticed . . .

Snowman

 **WRITER'S TECHNIQUE** Describing a character.

INTRODUCE

Introduce elaborative detail, reminding students about sensory detail. A fun way to begin the lesson is to gather pictures of several snowmen and write a descriptive paragraph about one in particular. The day of the lesson, post the pictures and read your paragraph—and see if students can match it to the right picture!

LITERATURE CONNECTION

Snowballs
by Lois Ehlert

The Snowman
by Raymond Briggs

MODEL

Ask the class to help you brainstorm ideas for describing a snowman; you can use the questions on the *Snowman* student page (p.31) to get going. Have a picture or model of a snowman for the class to work from (the more the better!), and chart as many responses as you get. Your chart might look something like this:

Size
huge, as tall as a tree, big as a house, towering over me

Shape
made of 3 big, round snowballs, the bottom one the biggest

Clothes
tattered red scarf, an itchy blue scarf, a tall black hat, fuzzy lime-green earmuffs, huge black sunglasses, a long purple stocking cap with a pompom, rainbow-colored mittens

Is he holding anything?
a snow shovel, a sled, a boom box

Eyes
sparkling blue marbles, black buttons, two red checkers, shiny copper pennies, coffee beans

Nose
a limp carrot, a small eggplant, a lightbulb, a rough black stone

Mouth
licorice, jelly beans, birdseed, coal

Arms
twigs, sticks, branches, paper-towel tubes

Choose the details you'd like, and translate them on the chart paper into complete sentences. Think aloud for students as you write your paragraph, which might look something like this:

The snowman was as tall as a towering pine tree! He was made of three round snowballs, the biggest one on the bottom. He wore a tattered red scarf and fuzzy green earmuffs. I was surprised at the huge black sunglasses that sat on his frosty white face. His arms were made of jaggedy twigs with rainbow-colored mittens covering the ends. I could barely see his sparkly blue-marble eyes behind his glasses, which sat above his lightbulb nose. I stared at his red licorice mouth, which was turned up in a smile. I smiled when I saw the sled that he pulled along beside him.

ART CONNECTION

MATERIALS
• blue construction paper
• white poster paint
• small sponges
• scissors
• white glue

Ask students to bring from home: felt, fabric scraps, buttons, raisins, popping corn, hard candy, toothpicks, cotton balls, cinnamon sticks, checkers, small stones, raffia, yarn, string, twigs, branches

PROCEDURE
1. Show students how to dab their sponges lightly in the paint and onto the page to create their snowman shapes.

2. When the paint dries, students can create their snowman's eyes, nose, and other features using the objects and scraps they brought from home and affixing them with glue.

3. While the snowmen dry, students can write their descriptive pieces. Then they can proofread them and copy them onto lined white paper cut into the shape of a snowman.

4. Students who finish early may go on to cut out a number of white snowflakes to grace a snowman bulletin board.

GUIDED PRACTICE

Once students have created their snowmen, have them answer the snowman questions based on their individual artwork. Then ask them to write down their ideas in paragraph form using the sentence starters.

Display Idea

Create a snowman bulletin board. You can post the snowmen on one side and the descriptions on the other, and then challenge students to match them up!

STUDENT SAMPLE

An amazing snowman stood by the pine tree. Ice coated snow covered him from head to toe. A bright red and blue scarf was wrapped tightly around his neck and blue earmuffs covered his ears. He had two black brass buttons for eyes that looked perfect with his liccorice mouth and slanted carrot nose. In his hand he held a wooden broom with hay bristles. He wore an open plaid shirt about his shoulders. As I looked more closely, I could almost see him smile at me on that cold winter day.

Name _____ Date _____

IMAGINE THAT . . .

You are trudging along a snowy mountain trail, and you come upon an amazing snowman!

Writer's Technique	Describing a character.
Artful Connection	Make your own fantastic snowman by sponging white paint on blue construction paper and adding trim and small objects from home.
Get Ready to Write!	Look at your amazing snowman. Then brainstorm answers to these questions to help you come up with terrific details about him. Be sure to include plenty of details!

How big is your snowman? _____

What shape is your snowman? _____

What is your snowman wearing? _____

What kind of arms does he have? _____

What kind of eyes does he have? _____

What kind of nose does he have? _____

What kind of mouth does he have? _____

Is he holding anything? _____

On another piece of paper, turn your ideas into complete sentences and arrange them into a paragraph. These sentence starters might help you.

I couldn't help but notice . . .

The snowman's _____ was . . .

His _____ seemed . . .

I smiled when I saw . . .

I was surprised at . . .

I stared at . . .

You couldn't miss . . .

He had . . .

Friendly Scarecrow

 **Describing a character.**

INTRODUCE

Introduce elaborative detail as a way to describe a character, showing students how specific details can reveal character traits. Tell them that you will be describing a *friendly* scarecrow.

MODEL

Show students how the questions on the *Friendly Scarecrow* student page (p 35) can help create a description of a character, reminding them that you want the scarecrow to be *friendly*. Having a picture or a photograph of a scarecrow on hand helps students generate lots of details. Chart as many responses as you get. Your chart might look something like this:

LITERATURE CONNECTION

Barn Dance
by Bill Martin, Jr. and
John Archambault

Scarecrow! by Valerie Littlewood

Feathertop by Rober D. San Souci

How big?

as tall as a pitchfork
way taller than me
taller than a cornstalk

Clothes

denim overalls
red plaid shirt
a big straw hat
dirty work gloves
old brown boots
a skirt and white apron

Holding anything?

a big, black crow
a corncob pipe
a rake
a bucket
a boom box

Eyes

drawn on an old sack of a face
    with a marker
stitched onto cloth
two radishes poked into
    a pumpkin head

Nose

a red triangle
a marshmallow on a toothpick
an old corncob
a cork

Mouth

a carved pumpkin frown
a red stitched smile
a green-bean grin

Hair

yellow straw
black yarn
corn silk
dried leaves

Head

a pumpkin
a stuffed pillowcase
a soccer ball

Stuffing

newspaper
dried leaves
straw and hay
sticks like bones to hold
    up arms, legs

After the class has finished brainstorming, ask them to help you choose the details that would make the scarecrow seem the most friendly. Record these on the chart paper in complete sentences, thinking aloud about how you craft the sentences to make your paragraph more than just a list of details. Your paragraph might look something like this:

I stared at the scarecrow, who stood as tall as the tallest cornstalk in the field! A pair of ragged denim overalls hugged his skinny body. A red plaid shirt covered his long arms and narrow chest. A pair of old, dirty work gloves hung from his sleeves and flapped about in the breeze. I could hardly take my eyes off the wide straw hat that perched on his head. Straggly corn-silk hair peeked out from beneath the hat. I smiled as I gazed into his merry, red-radish eyes and dried-up corncob nose. His head was a huge, round pumpkin with a wide, toothless grin carved out. He seemed to be stuffed with hay, which sprouted out here and there.

ART CONNECTION

MATERIALS
- manila construction paper
- construction paper in assorted colors
- crayons, markers
- scissors
- glue
- oaktag
- Ask students to bring from home: felt, fabric scraps, buttons, raisins, popping corn, small stones, raffia, yarn, string, twigs, dried leaves, grasses, straw, hay, cornstalks

PROCEDURE
1. Show students how to lightly sketch a scarecrow. Be sure to fill a large-sized paper.

2. Demonstrate how to cut scraps of paper and/or fabric in the shape of various articles of clothing—hat, shoes, etc. Add small detail items. (You might want to provide blunt knitting needles and yarn for students to "stitch" around the edges of their scarecrow's clothing.)

3. Have students glue their scarecrows onto a large piece of oaktag.

GUIDED PRACTICE

Once students have created their scarecrows, they can answer the questions on the student page and compose their descriptive paragraph. Remind them that they're describing a *friendly* scarecrow. Circulate as they work, offering direction and encouragement. When students are satisfied with their pieces, have them copy them onto lined white paper.

Try This!
Bind the scarecrows with their companion descriptions together into a class book titled *Scarecrow Field Guide* or *Have You Ever Seen This Scarecrow?*

STUDENT SAMPLE

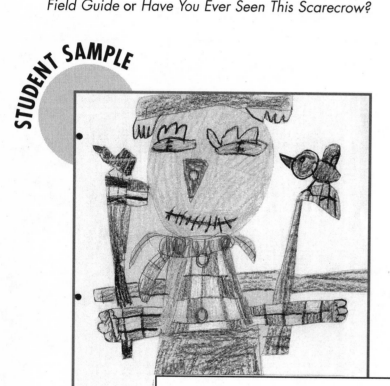

His shirt covered his straw body. Sitting on his head was a brown straw hat. A purple and orange scarf flew over his neck. His bunching overalls covered his black and husky boots. His mouth was stitched up like a blanket. He had stitched up eyes too. A red and white flag blew back and forth as the wind blew. Black furry gloves were dangling off his arms. As I crept closer I realized it was a scarecrow.

Name _____ Date _____

IMAGINE THAT . . .

▏▎

One autumn afternoon you are taking a stroll beside a cornfield, and you see a scarecrow waving at you!

Writer's Technique   Describing a character.

Artful Connection   Design your own friendly scarecrow using a variety of paper, fabric, yarn, and other natural materials (corn husks, dried grass and leaves, hay, etc.).

Get Ready to Write!   Look at the scarecrow you have created. Then brainstorm answers to these questions. They will help you come up with terrific details to make your friendly scarecrow come alive. Be specific!

How big is your scarecrow? _____

What kind of hair does your scarecrow have? _____

What is your scarecrow wearing? _____

What is your scarecrow made out of/stuffed with? _____

What kind of eyes does he/she have? _____

What kind of nose does he/she have? _____

What kind of mouth does he/she have? _____

Is he/she holding anything? _____

On another piece of paper, turn your ideas into complete sentences. These sentence starters might help you.

. . . covered his/her . . .   You couldn't miss his/her . . .

A . . . hugged his/her . . .   He/She wore a . . .

The scarecrow's . . . was . . .   I smiled when I saw . . .

I could barely take my eyes off his/her . . .   He/She had . . .

Describing a character.

INTRODUCE

Introduce elaborative detail as a way to describe a character, reminding students how you used specific details to create a friendly scarecrow.

MODEL

Use the questions on the *Pirate* student page (p.39) to elicit ideas from the class for describing the
pirate. Whereas in the scarecrow activity you were aiming for a friendly character, here students
can choose what kind of pirate their character will be, so encourage a wide range of responses.
Working from a picture of a pirate helps inspire students. Record student responses on chart
paper. Your chart might look something like this:

How Tall?
about my height
tall as a giant
towering over me

Eyes?
beady
dark eyes
twinkling blue eyes
merry brown eyes
burning blue eyes

Nose?
short, stubby
long, hooked
sharp as a sword

What kind of expression?
jolly smile
shocked
wide-eyed
mean, sneering
playful
mischievous

Hair?
wild black hair
bald, shiny head
short, curly red
hair

What Clothes?
red knickers
black pants
red-striped shirt
velvet coat
three-cornered hat
red bandanna
black shoes with gold buckles
gold hoop in one ear
eye patch
peg leg

Holding?
a sword
a treasure chest
a cutlass
a big sack
a parrot

Sound?
grumbling
huffing and puffing
whistling a sea
chantey

How does this character make you feel?
terrified
excited
nervous
shocked
happy

Ask students to choose an adjective to describe the pirate—*scary, jolly, friendly, mean*—and discuss what about his appearance would make them think that. Then choose details that will show readers that the pirate is, say, *jolly*; you may want to highlight or underline them on your chart, as we have done below. Translate those details into complete sentences on the chart paper, being sure to think aloud for students as you go. Your paragraph might look something like this:

I gaped at the huge pirate standing before me. He wore <u>red knickers</u> and a fancy <u>black-velvet jacket</u> and ruffled shirt. A <u>three-cornered hat</u> covered his <u>wild black hair.</u> I could hardly take my eyes off his <u>shiny black shoes</u> with square <u>golden buckles.</u> I was shocked at the sight of his <u>burning blue eyes</u> and the <u>mischievous smile</u> below a thick, curled moustache. His nose was <u>long and hooked, sharp as the sword</u> that hung by his side. In his hand, he held a cage with a <u>large, brightly colored parrot</u> inside. He whistled a <u>sea chantey,</u> which made me feel as jolly as he looked!

ART CONNECTION

MATERIALS
- oaktag (for templates, if desired)
- manila construction paper
- markers
- crayons
- construction paper in assorted colors
- scissors
- glue
- brass fasteners

PREPARATION
If desired, you may prepare templates of a pirate's head, torso, and limbs on oaktag for students to trace. (The torso and head should be one piece.)

PROCEDURE
1. First, students create the body of their pirate, either by tracing the head, torso, and limbs onto manila paper or drawing them freehand. (The head and torso should be one piece and the limbs should be drawn separately; they are attached in Step 4.)

2. Next, students color in clothing and facial features.

3. They may cut out hats and other accessories from construction paper scraps and glue them on.

4. Finally, they cut out the arms and legs and attach the limbs to the torso with brass fasteners.

Try This!

Have students bring in a plain brown-paper grocery bag from home. Tear a rough rectangular shape (approximately 12" x 10") and crumple it to simulate an old parchment treasure map. Discuss possible map symbols—footsteps, skull and crossbones, palm trees, and, of course, an "X" marking the treasure spot! Create a map key and have students draw their map with black markers. Display maps beside their pirates.

GUIDED PRACTICE

Once students have created their own pirate, invite them to answer the questions on the student page. Then they can write their ideas down using the sentence starters and create their own descriptive paragraphs. Remind them to capture the *feeling* the pirate evokes in them with their details. (Option: Give students a lead sentence to begin with: *I gaped at the pirate standing before me!*) When students are satisfied with their pieces, invite them to copy them over onto clean paper for display.

Try This!

You can offer students a choice—they can create and write about pirates *or* mermaids. The procedure is the same. You'll just need to slightly modify the questioning.

Display Idea

Put pirates on a bulletin board, accompanied by treasure maps and chests!

STUDENT SAMPLE

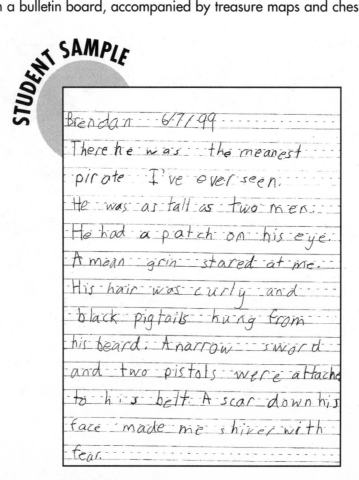

Brendan   6/7/99

There he was the meanest pirate I've ever seen. He was as tall as two men. He had a patch on his eye. A mean grin stared at me. His hair was curly and black pigtails hung from his beard. A narrow sword and two pistols were attached to his belt. A scar down his face made me shiver with fear.

Name _____ Date _____

IMAGINE THAT . . .

||||||||||||||||||||||||||||||||||||||||||||||||||||||||||||||||||||||||||||||||||||

While strolling along a deserted beach, you catch sight of an incredible character . . . a pirate!

Writer's Technique   Describing a character.

Artful Connection   Draw a pirate on a large piece of paper. Cut out and glue on a variety of construction paper clothing, hair, and whatever the pirate may be holding in his/her hands.

Get Ready to Write!   Study your pirate. Then brainstorm answers to these questions that will help you come up with terrific details about your character. Be specific!

How tall is your pirate? _____

What is your pirate wearing? _____

What kind of hair does the pirate have? _____

What kind of eyes does he/she have? _____

What kind of nose does he/she have? _____

What kind of expression is on your pirate's face? _____

Is he/she making any sounds? _____

Is he/she holding anything? _____

How does the pirate make you feel? _____

On another paper, turn your ideas into complete sentences. These sentence starters might help you.

I gaped at . . .	I was shocked at the sight of . . .
His/Her hair . . .	Looking closely, I saw . . .
The pirate's . . . was . . .	Gazing at him/her, I noticed . . .
I could barely take my eyes off his/her . . .	In his/her hands was . . .
A . . . covered his/her . . .	Just looking at him/her made me feel . .
He/She wore a . . .	My heart pounded as I realized . . .

Jungle Creature

 **WRITER'S TECHNIQUE** > ## Describing an animal.

INTRODUCE

Introduce elaborative detail as a way to describe animals. This can be a great link to any habitat study. You could invite students to research various animals and then write about one that interests them most.

LITERATURE CONNECTION

Rainforest Animals by Paul Hess

The Great Kapok Tree
by Lynne Cherry

A Walk in the Rainforest
by Kristin Joy Pratt

The Grouchy Ladybug
and *The Very Busy Spider*
by Eric Carle

MODEL

Demonstrate how the questions on the *Jungle Creature* student page (p. 43) can help you think up details for a jungle animal. Have several books and/or pictures that illustrate a variety of colorful jungle animals for the students to consult. Together, choose a particular animal to describe, explaining that students will be able to choose their own animals later. Encourage students to brainstorm as many details as possible. One class chose to describe a leopard, and their chart looked like this:

Leopard

How big is the leopard?

jumbo cat
the size of a dozen house cats
way bigger than our family dog
large, powerful

What kind of fur?

short, golden fur with black spots
sleek, shiny, yellow fur

What kind of legs?

four muscular legs
powerful legs ready to pounce

What kind of ears and tail?

small triangle ears
cat ears
long, flicking tail
thin, spotted tail

What kind of eyes does it have?

green, glowing
golden, slanty
dark, cautious

What kind of snout does it have?

black nose with long whiskers

What kind of mouth does it have?

wide mouth
long, pink tongue
sharp, pointy white teeth . . .

How does it move?

smoothly, gracefully
quietly
like a hunter

What kinds of sounds does it make?

low growl, raspy meow,
soft rumble

Choose the details you'd like from the chart, thinking aloud about how you made your choices. Then work them into a paragraph on chart paper; it might look something like this:

I stared at the beautiful beast in the clearing. It was much larger than the family dog, sleek and powerful. It was hard to tear my eyes away from its shiny, golden fur dotted with small patches of black. This magnificent creature stood on four powerful legs, which looked ready to pounce. I smiled as I noticed its small, pointy ears and long tail, which flicked back and forth like a house cat's. The leopard stared at me with its green, glowing eyes and sniffed the air with its black nose and quivering whiskers. I was surprised at the graceful way the leopard moved through the underbrush. Just then, a low, rumbling sound sent a shiver down my spine. It was the sound of the leopard purring as it slunk off into the jungle.

ART CONNECTION

Have students sketch their animals, then glue on overlapping tissue paper in various complementary shades, mosaic style. Add details with black marker. (These should be reminiscent of Eric Carle's artwork; see literature connection [p.40] for titles.)

MATERIALS

- white or manila construction paper
- white glue
- paintbrushes
- paper plates
- tissue paper in assorted colors
- scissors
- fine-line black markers

PROCEDURE

1. Show students how to sketch their creatures using a variety of basic shapes to create the basic outline. Encourage them to fill the better part of an 8½" x 11" sheet of white or manila paper.

2. Next, mix a thick solution of glue and water to a consistency that can be easily spread with a paintbrush. Place a paper-plateful of glue solution near each group of students.

3. Show students how to tear small pieces of tissue paper in various shades of similar colors, place them over their animal sketch, and paint over with glue solution. Each piece should overlap the last. There is no need to worry about staying within the lines—the lines will show through the layers of tissue paper, and once dry, students will simply cut out their animals, leaving only clean edges.

4. After their collage creatures are dry, students may add details—spots, stripes, claws, fangs, feathers—with a fine-line black marker.

GUIDED PRACTICE

When students finish the tissue-paper representation of their chosen animal, ask them to answer the questions on the student page. Then ask them to write their ideas down using the sentence starters, creating a complete descriptive paragraph. (Option: Give students a lead sentence to begin: *I stared at the beautiful beast in the clearing.*)

Display Idea

Display jungle creatures and descriptive pieces together on a bulletin board decorated with large clumps of jungle grasses, vines, and exotic flowers and trees (cut from construction paper).

STUDENT SAMPLE

There I was, on an interactive jungle safari in Australia. I ventured farther into the jungle world to explore more of its amazing winding rivers and exotic plants. Suddenly, a long, thin snake slithered out of the shallow river. I was stunned. I never thought I would encounter such a large reptile. I tensed, but relaxed as I soon realized that the snake had no intention of harming me. I recognized the creature as a water Python because of its unique features. It was about seven feet long, with a slender body. Its smooth, scaly skin was a dark brown with a bright-yellow underside. The snake had a large, irregular head with some markings, scars, and cuts. Its tiny, pure-black eyes never seemed to close. One of this python's most interesting facial features was its whitish lips with a powdered effect. The python's teeth frightened me most of all. They were sharp, long fangs that could grasp onto anything and remain in the same tight position. He seemed to sulk and then gracefully slip into the water, leaving me open-mouthed and speechless.

Jungle Creature Student Page

Name _____ Date _____

IMAGINE THAT . . .

While on a jungle safari, you encounter an exotic creature—a tiger, leopard, monkey, parrot, giant snake . . . the wilder the better!

Writer's Technique   Describing an animal.

Artful Connection   Make your own jungle creature using brightly colored tissue paper. Sketch your creature on manila paper, then tear small pieces of tissue paper and glue them down until your entire creature is covered.

Get Ready to Write!   Brainstorm answers to these questions that will help you come up with terrific details about your creature.

How big is your creature? _____

What kind of fins, fur, feathers, or skin does it have? _____

What kind of legs does it have? _____

What kind of wings, ears, tail does it have? _____

What kind of eyes does it have? _____

What kind of nose/snout/beak does it have? _____

What kind of mouth/teeth/tongue does it have? _____

How does it move? _____

What kinds of sounds does it make? _____

On another paper, turn your ideas into complete sentences, using these sentence starters to help you.

This furry/feathered/scaly beast had . . .   I was amazed at . . .

I was surprised at . . .   This magnificent animal's . . .

The creature's . . . was . . .   I smiled when I noticed . . .

I stared at . . .   It was hard to tear my eyes away from its . . .

Gingerbread House

 **Describe an object.**

INTRODUCE

Introduce elaborative detail as a way of describing a story-critical object. This is a great time to review story-critical elements; you could ask students to brainstorm situations in which a gingerbread house would be a story-critical object.

LITERATURE CONNECTION

The Gingerbread Baby
by Jan Brett

The Gingerbread Boy
by Paul Galdone

Holiday magazines often have great pictures of gingerbread figures.

MODEL

Model using the questions from the *Gingerbread House* student page (p. 47) to get ideas for describing a gingerbread house. A few pictures of gingerbread houses, or an actual one, can provide students with the necessary background from which they can generate their responses. This is a great activity for using smell and taste, the two senses most often neglected in student writing. Chart all responses students give; your chart might look something like this:

How big is the gingerbread house?

small, cozy
huge, 3-story house

What color are the walls?

soft brown
warm tan color
the color of cookies

What kind of windows and doors?

rock-candy windows
chocolate-bar doors
jelly bean stained-glass windows

What kind of roof does it have?

shingled in M&M's
layered in peppermints

What kind of shutters?

huge, gum-stick shutters
taffy shutters
licorice shutters

What kind of steps and porch does it have?

steps made of butterscotch candies
a porch lined with shoestring licorice

How does it smell?

chocolatey
minty
butterscotch

How does it taste?

like candy bars
like spicy gingerbread
like sugar coating

Choose the details you'd like, and use them to compose a paragraph on chart paper, thinking aloud for the class. Your paragraph might look something like this:

I smiled as I laid eyes on the small, cozy, gingerbread cottage. The walls were the warm-brown color of just-baked cookies. My mouth watered at the sight of the rock-candy windows and doors made of shiny, bright hard candies. I could hardly believe the pink taffy shutters beside each window and the red-and-white-striped peppermint roof. I stared at the butterscotch steps and licorice-lined porch, and my stomach growled. As I crept up closer, I noticed a sweet, spicy smell. I ran my finger along the side of the house and licked it. Ummmm … sugar coating!

ART CONNECTION

MATERIALS
- oaktag (optional)
- brown cardboard
- scissors
- crayons
- cake icing in a tube
- tacky glue
- Ask students to bring in: cardboard (if you can't provide it), a variety of small candies or cake trimmings—hard candies, M&M's, licorice, jelly beans, mints (anything that will not easily melt)

PREPARATION
If desired, make a number of house templates (squares for walls, rectangles and triangles for roofs, etc.) out of oaktag for students to trace.

PROCEDURE
1. Students design their house, either tracing templates for the various parts (walls and roof) or creating their own shapes on cardboard.

2. If possible, have students cut out the pieces. If the cardboard is too thick or cumbersome, you may need to take home the sheets in advance and cut them with an X-acto™ knife.

3. Ask students to sketch in doors, windows, shutters, chimneys, and other house details and then outline these details in bold crayon colors.

4. Help students trim their houses with a thin line of white frosting (which will harden as it is exposed to the air).

5. Students place their candies strategically over their sketch and then glue them down.

Try This!

An alternate activity involves saving cafeteria-size individual milk cartons and covering them with graham crackers for a 3-D gingerbread house. Fill seams with icing in a tube. Glue on candy for doors, windows, roof, etc.

GUIDED PRACTICE

Once students have designed and built their gingerbread houses, ask them to describe their houses, using the prompts and sentence starters on the student page. Walk among students as they work, offering advice and encouragement as needed.

Display Idea

Make a gingerbread village!

STUDENT SAMPLE

Emily

I gasped so loud I thought my chest would pop. My mouth fell open. I lept for joy in the air and screamed. How could I help it? Right in front of my own two eyes was a giant gingerbread house! Thick, frosted, sugar paned window glass sparkled like magic in the sun's golden light. The rich chocolate outside walls looked so creamy and deleicious. Perfect shaped gumdrops lined the sugar roof in neat rows so they were squeezed so tightly there was not a single crack. Pepermints sered an elegant chimney and deep mouth watering smells came from deep down inside to who knows where. The door was made up of nothing but swirly crusty cinnamon sticks. A wonderful smell came wafting to my nostrils. Fruity, chewy,

Starbursts lead a brightly colored path to the house that remind me of a rainbow; after the rain.

Gingerbread House

Name _____ Date _____

IMAGINE THAT...

You are strolling through a part of the forest you have never been to before, and you come to a clearing. In the center stands a gingerbread house covered in candy!

Writer's Technique   Describing an object.

Artful Connection   Make your own gingerbread house out of cardboard and small candies! Be sure to include plenty of details—windows, doors, chimneys, and plenty of trim.

Get Ready to Write!   Look carefully at your gingerbread house. Then brainstorm answers to these questions that will help you come up with terrific details about your house.

How big is your house? _____

What color are the walls? _____

What kind of windows, doors, shutters does it have? _____

What kind of roof does it have? _____

What kind of steps/porch does it have? _____

What kind of shingles does it have? _____

What do you smell near the house? _____

If you nibbled at the house, what might you taste? _____

On another piece of paper, turn your ideas into complete sentences. These sentence starters might help you.

The scrumptious cottage had . . .

I was delighted with . . .

I stared at . . .

I could hardly believe the . . .

Its doors/windows/shutters were made of . . .

It was hard to tear my eyes away from its . . .

I smiled when I noticed . . .

My mouth watered at the sight of . . .

My stomach growled when I saw . . .

Ancient Crown

Describing an object.

INTRODUCE

You can begin a discussion about crowns by asking students what type of people wear crowns and referring to characters from literature. Gathering a collection of both real and storybook crowns to share with the class makes an effective introduction.

LITERATURE CONNECTION

The King Rains
by Fred Gwynne

King Bidgood's in the Bathtub
by Audrey and Don Woods

MODEL

Ask students to close their eyes and visualize a fancy crown for an ancient king or queen. Then ask them the questions from the *Ancient Crown* student page (p.51), recording their answers on chart paper.

What is the crown made of?
shiny gold, polished silver, glittering glass, heavy glowing metal

What is the texture of the crown?
smooth and worn, rough and grooved, carved designs on it, polished and slippery

How old do you think it might be?
ancient, 500 years, from the days of the knights

What color is the crown?
reflects rainbow colors, gold and silver, trimmed in white fur

How heavy is it?
as heavy as a dictionary, light as a feather, the same as a baseball cap

What is it shaped like?
rounded edges, pointy peaks around the edge, scalloped top, zigzagged in the front

What is it decorated with?
green emeralds, dazzling rubies, round white pearls, rainbow-colored jewels, polished stones

Whom do you think it belonged to?
a famous king, a wise queen, a brave prince, a courageous princess

Think aloud as you choose details and turn them into a paragraph on chart paper. Your paragraph might look something like this:

The incredible crown seemed to be made out of gold and silver, the color of a sunset. The rim was rounded where it sat against your head, and the opposite edge was shaped into pointy peaks. I stared at the shiny jewels, every color of the rainbow, that decorated its smooth, shiny surface. Around the edges were rows of small, round white pearls. When I picked it up, I realized it was quite heavy, and, looking closely, I could see that it was very old, probably from the days of knights and castles. Perhaps it was once worn by a brave king or a courageous princess.

ART CONNECTION

MATERIALS
- oaktag
- scissors
- stapler
- markers
- glitter, beads, sequins, etc.
- tacky glue
- cotton

PREPARATION
Cut oaktag strips 21" x 5" for each student. (Using the paper cutter is easiest.) If desired, create templates of patterns for crown edges.

PROCEDURE
1. Distribute strips and have students pencil in the upper edge of their crowns and cut them out, using templates if desired.

2. Have students turn their strips on the wrong side and write in their royal name: for example, *Queen Marissa, Prince Kevin.*

3. Invite students to decorate their crowns with markers. Set out the glitter, sequins, and beads; students can decorate with these using tacky glue. Glue on cotton (or polyfill) to simulate an ermine fur trim. Use a black marker to dot ermine fur.

4. Size each crown around each student's head and staple to fit.

"What a remarkable crown!" I screamed. Gold and silver dazzled in the light. It was as yellow as the sun and as white as the snow. A ring of emeralds and strangely shaped crystals decorated it. It was probably 1,000 years old. The back looked like mountain peaks, and the front was round. It was as heavy as a ten-pound weight. I wonder if it belonged to a prince, I thought.

GUIDED PRACTICE

Once students have decorated their crowns, have them complete the questions on the student page and compose their descriptive paragraphs.

Presentation Idea

As a fun wrap-up activity, invite students to wear their crowns and read their paragraphs to the class.

Name _____ Date _____

IMAGINE THAT...

While exploring a medieval castle, you discover a big, fancy crown!

Writer's Technique   Describing an object.

Artful Connection   Make your own crown out of oaktag and glitter! Be sure to include plenty of fancy details by gluing on small sequins, beads, and plastic jewels.

Get Ready to Write!   After you've created your own fancy crown, look at it carefully. Then brainstorm answers to these questions that will help you come up with terrific details about your crown.

What is your crown made out of? _____

What color(s) is it? _____

What is it shaped like? _____

What is its texture? _____

What is it decorated with? _____

How heavy is it? _____

How old would you guess it is? _____

Whom do you suppose it belonged to? _____

On another piece of paper, turn your ideas into complete sentences. These sentence starters might help you.

The incredible crown had . . .   I loved the . . .

It was the color of . . .   It was decorated with . . .

It seemed to be made of . . .   When I picked it up, I realized . . .

I stared at . . .   It must have been . . .

Around the edges were . . .   Perhaps it belonged to . . .

Suspense

One way that authors capture their readers' attention is by using suspense. Whenever an author withholds information, hints about—but does not reveal—what is coming next, or raises questions or worries, the audience becomes hooked!

WORD REFERENTS

How can we build suspense? One easy way is through the use of *word referents*. Instead of naming the character, the author refers to him or her through indefinite references, called word referents. Then, after revealing hints about the character, little by little, the character is named—the revelation. See how this works in the following paragraph:

LITERATURE CONNECTION

The BFG
by Roald Dahl

Suddenly
by Colin McNaughton

I stepped into the clearing and froze. I couldn't believe my eyes! **The tiny being** was short and squatty, but powerfully built. **He** wore brightly colored but ragged clothes and held a club in his fists. I stared at the **tiny man's** long, straggly hair and crooked teeth and gasped. It was a troll!

Notice how the author begins with strong emotions that cause the reader to wonder what the main character is seeing. A description follows using word referents. Finally, the revelation is made. This is much more effective than stating: *I stepped into the clearing and saw a troll!*

THE MAGIC OF THREE

Another way to build suspense is through the *Magic of Three*. The author sets up a series of three hints, which lead to a discovery. The plot follows this basic pattern:

HINT #1:

The main character detects something amiss. (Perhaps hears a strange noise, sees something out of the corner of his/her eye—the hint can involve any of the five senses.) But nothing is discovered. The main character reacts, probably dismissing the clue as just his or her imagination.

HINT #2:

The main character detects a second clue, this time something different, involving another of the five senses. Again, nothing is discovered. The main character exhibits a more intense reaction.

HINT #3:

The main character detects a third clue, this one leading to a discovery or revelation. Watch how this strategy works in the following example.

There I was, creeping through Grandpa's basement. Suddenly, I heard a rustling sound in the corner. I peered into the shadows but didn't see a thing. I shrugged and moved on. The next thing I knew, I saw something out of the corner of my eye. I spun around, but couldn't find anything unusual. My heart began to pound, and I rushed toward the stairs. That was when I felt something cool and clammy brush up against me. I gasped! It was a ghost!

SO, THE PATTERN FOR THE MAGIC OF THREE IS:

HINT #1
• You observe or sense something.
• You discover nothing.
• You react.

HINT #2
• You observe or sense something else.
• You discover nothing.
• You react.

HINT #3
• You observe or sense something else.
• You make your discovery.
• You react.

These techniques not only capture and keep the reader's attention—they also add real entertainment value to the story and are great fun for both the author and the audience!

Who's Inside the Mitten?

Building suspense with word referents.

INTRODUCE

A fun way to introduce suspense with word referents is to bring in a mitten with a small stuffed animal or figurine hidden inside. Describe what's in the mitten, giving hints and revealing key attributes of object. Invite students to guess what it is, and pull it out with a flourish for your revelation!

LITERATURE CONNECTION

The Mitten
by Jan Brett

MODEL

Make an overhead of the passage on page 52. Then read it aloud as the students follow along. When you finish, ask students to go back and pick out words that stood for the troll; underline *tiny being, he,* and *tiny man* as students call them out. Now's a good time to introduce the term *word referent* and to create a model paragraph with the class that uses this technique.

Start by writing a lead sentence that sets a purpose for the action: *Just then, I saw the mitten lying in the freshly fallen snow.* Ask students to choose an animal to hide in the mitten, encouraging them to select one they're familiar with so they have a lot of information to draw on for their description. In our community, a favorite example to use is a skunk.

Now ask students to think about what kinds of hints they could give: size, color, eyes, ears, tail, etc. Here are the questions and answers one class came up with for a skunk:

How big is the animal?

(*not in inches but relative to something else the audience might be familiar with*)
it was about twice the size
    of a cat
as big as a poodle
an oversized rat

What kind and color of fur?

sleek black fur
shiny fur
white stripe down middle
    of back

What kind of eyes did it have?

small, black beady eyes
soft brown eyes
little shifty eyes

What kind of ears did it have?

small round discs
blended into head

What was its tail like?

long, thick tail
bushy
curled

What words could you use to refer to the animal?

the creature
the furry friend
the cuddly critter
the small rodent
the menace
it

Now model turning the answers to the questions into a suspenseful paragraph, using plenty of description and word referents that won't give the animal away. Here's our sample paragraph for the skunk:

Just then, I saw the mitten lying in the freshly fallen snow. I looked inside. I could not believe my eyes! It was about the size of a large house cat. The creature's small, black beady eyes stared cautiously at me. As I looked more closely, I noticed its sleek black fur and small ears. The critter had a long, bushy tail that was tightly curled around its body. A chill ran down my spine when I noticed the thick white stripe that ran down its back. It was a skunk!

ART CONNECTION

MATERIALS
- mitten template (optional)
- construction paper in assorted colors (each student will need two 8½" x 11" sheets)
- crayons, markers
- scissors
- yarn
- large blunt knitting needle, sewing needle or hole punch
- white or manila construction paper
- glue, tape

PREPARATION
Prepare a mitten template for students to trace, if desired.

PROCEDURE
1. Distribute the construction paper. Ask students to draw or trace two identical mittens and cut them out. Encourage them to use as much of the paper as possible. To ensure that the mittens will match, students can tape two sheets of paper together, draw one mitten, and cut it out through both sheets.

2. After they have cut out the mittens, students should place one on top of the other, being careful to line up the edges.

3. Distribute yarn to everyone, and tell them that they will be "sewing" the mitten together. They should leave an opening at the wrist so that when they are finished, they will have created a pocket. (Students can use a blunt knitting needle to thread the yarn around the edges, or you can hole-punch the edges of the mitten and have the students thread the yarn through the holes.)

4. After students are finished sewing their mitten, give them a small piece of white or manila construction paper to draw their creature on. Tell them to check to see if it will fit inside the mitten. Encourage them to use lots of detail.

GUIDED PRACTICE

Once students have decided upon what animal will take up residence in their mittens, invite them to write a paragraph that builds suspense about what is actually inside, using word referents. The questions on the *Who's Inside the Mitten* student page (p.57) will help them get started, and the final sentence should reveal the animal.

Display Idea

Have students insert their "revelation" into the mitten and glue their written suspense piece to the outside; then post them on the bulletin board. Invite another class in to guess what's in the mittens!

STUDENT SAMPLE

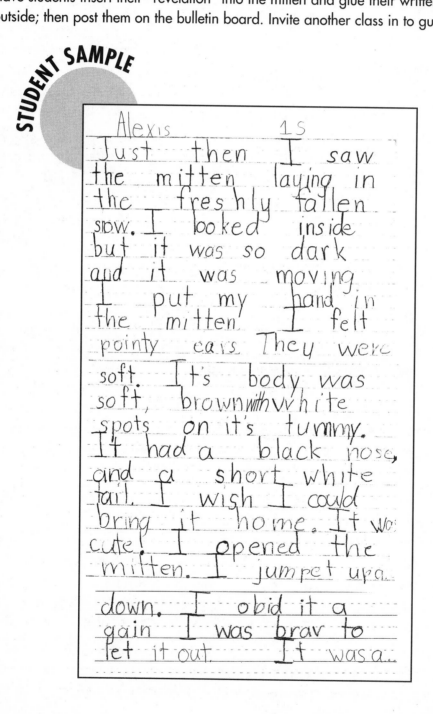

Alexis   15

Just then I saw the mitten laying in the freshly fallen snow. I looked inside but it was so dark and it was moving. I put my hand in the mitten. I felt pointy ears. They were soft. It's body was soft, brown with white spots on it's tummy. It had a black nose, and a short white tail. I wish I could bring it home. It was cute! I opened the mitten. I jumpet up a down. I obid it a gain. I was brav to let it out. It was a...

Who's Inside the Mitten? Student Page

Name _____ Date _____

IMAGINE THAT . . .

You are outside on a cold winter day. You just lost your mitten and are looking for it. Suddenly, you see it. As you reach for it, it starts to move! You pick up the mitten and look inside. You are surprised to see an animal!

Artful Connection Make a mitten out of construction paper and put your revelation inside. On the outside, paste your suspenseful writing piece so that everyone can take turns guessing.

Writer's Technique Building suspense with word referents.

Here is how you can use word referents to build suspense:

- List all the things that you could call your animal without saying what it is. For example: *the tiny creature, the little beast, my furry friend.*
- When you write your paragraph, use these word referents instead of naming the animal. Save your revelation for the end!

Get Ready to Write!

1. Think about animals that live in woodland, prairie, or mountain habitats. Choose an animal that you know a lot about.

2. Brainstorm the characteristics or qualities your animal has, remembering to use your five senses. What does your animal look like? What sounds does it make? Does it have a particular smell? What would it feel like if you petted it? How does it move?

3. Write a paragraph (4–5 sentences) that makes your reader wonder about the creature that's hidden in your mitten. Use word referents to build suspense, remember to include sensory details, and reveal your creature in the last sentence!

_____

_____

_____

_____

_____

Who's Gobbling?

 **WRITER'S TECHNIQUE** ▶ **Building Suspense with the Magic of Three.**

INTRODUCE

Introduce building suspense with the Magic of Three. If your students are not familiar with wild turkeys, be sure to read about or discuss their habitat, appearance, and behavior, providing enough background knowledge for students to apply to their writing.

LITERATURE CONNECTION

Turkeys That Fly and Turkeys That Don't
by Allan Fowler

A Turkey for Thanksgiving
by Eve Bunting

MODEL

Model the Magic of Three pattern using the example on page 53. Read the paragraph together, and then ask students to pick out the three hints and reactions and identify the revelation. Next, walk students through the activity on the *Who's Gobbling?* student page (p. 61).

Give students a lead sentence that sets a purpose for the action:
> *One autumn afternoon I strolled along through the forest.*

Give students the discovery with which to end their suspenseful paragraph:
> *There, staring up at me, was a wild turkey!*

Then ask students about what kinds of clues they might encounter, prompting them to use the five senses. Questions might include:

- What might you **HEAR** if a turkey was running through the underbrush?
  a shuffling sound, rustling leaves, snapping twigs, gobbling (suggest that student save this for their last hint!)

- What might you **SEE** if a turkey ran past into the underbrush, just out of view?
  a blur, a streak of brown and red, a shadow, something in the corner of your eye, a feather

- What might you **SENSE OR FEEL** if a wild turkey was nearby?
  a feeling of being watched, something rubbing against your leg

- How would you **REACT** to each of these hints?
  nervous, heart pounding, you quicken your step, a shiver down your spine, hands tremble, knees feel weak, you begin to sweat, you gasp, look around, listen closely

- What **"RED FLAG"** words might you use to grab the reader's attention for each new hint?
  suddenly, all of a sudden, just then, the next thing I knew, before I knew it

Think aloud for the class as you craft student responses into the Magic of Three pattern on chart paper. Your paragraph might look something like this:

One autumn afternoon, I strolled along through the forest. Suddenly, there was a rustling sound in the bushes along the path. I paused and looked around, and my heart began to beat a little faster. There was nothing there. I shrugged and walked on, a little faster this time. Just then, I saw something out of the corner of my eye—just a quick flash of brown and red. I whirled about, but again, there was nothing out of the ordinary. Feeling a little nervous, my knees turning to jelly, I went on, determined to get out of the woods as quickly as I could. The next thing I knew, I heard a loud gobbling sound. I gasped. There, staring up at me, was a wild turkey!

GUIDED PRACTICE

For this activity, it's not necessary to complete the art component first, although it will help focus students on their main event. Students can write their own Magic of Three suspense paragraph, working from your modeled paragraph and the outline on the student page.

ART CONNECTION

MATERIALS

- plastic cups (preferably red, but any color will do), one for each student
- scissors
- string
- construction paper in assorted colors
- crayons, markers
- glue, tape

PREPARATION

1. Use sharp end of scissors (or other pointed implement) to puncture a small hole in the center of the bottom of each cup. (The hole should be just large enough to thread the string through; see Step 1.)

2. Cut a 12" length of string for each student. (Or have them measure and cut their own in class.)

3. If desired, create templates of feathers and a turkey head for students to trace.

PROCEDURE

1. Distribute cups and string. Instruct students to tie a large knot at one end of their string. Ask them to place the cups open-end-down on their desks and thread the unknotted end of their string through the hole in their cups. They should pull the string through so that it hangs beneath the cup, as shown in Step 2.

2. Pass out small pieces of brown construction paper for the turkey's head. Ask the children to draw a turkey head shape—having a picture available is a great help! (The variations in students' interpretation of this produces a unique flock of turkeys! For a more consistent result, you may cut templates for students, out of oaktag.) See Step 3.

3. Students then draw in eyes, a beak, and a snood, the loose flap of skin that hangs over the beak. Tape the head to the cup.

4. Now students cut out five construction-paper feathers as shown. (Again, you may have them draw and cut their own or use a template.) They may add crayon shading and detail. Finally, arrange them to the cup as shown in Step 4 and tape in place.

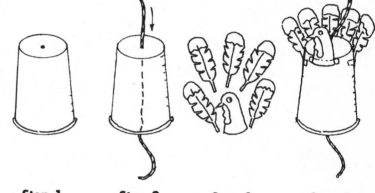

Step 1   **Step 2**   **Step 3**   **Step 4**

Try This!

Now comes the fun part! Have students wet the fingers of one hand and hold their turkey gobblers in the other. Have them tug at the string with wet fingers. This produces an amazing gobbling sound!

Presentation Idea

Invite students to work in pairs, one reading aloud the suspense piece while the other creates sounds effect with the plastic-cup gobblers.

STUDENT SAMPLE

As I walked through the woods, I could hear leaves crunching and crackling underneath my feet. Suddenly, I heard something behind a tall oak tree; it sounded like shaking feathers. I was too scared to look. I didn't hear anything else, so I figured it was just the wind blowing on the leaves. I walked a few more feet when I thought I saw a gigantic feather on the ground a little bit ahead. I crept ahead to take a look. The feather turned out to be a twig, but I still felt uneasy. I spun around as I heard a branch snap, and found myself standing face o face with a wild turkey! whew!

Who's Gobbling? Student Page

Name _____ Date _____

IMAGINE THAT . . .

You are strolling through the forest on an autumn day when suddenly you realize that you are not alone. Someone or something is nearby! You wonder what it is, but you discover nothing. You move on, and, for the second time, there is some hint—something you hear, see, or sense—that tells you something is near. Once again, nothing seems out of the ordinary, but you begin to feel nervous. You walk on, and a third time you are made aware that you are not alone. You finally discover what has been lurking in the underbrush—you find yourself facing a gobbling wild turkey!

Writer's Technique   Building suspense with the Magic of Three.

Here is the pattern that writers follow to build suspense using the Magic of Three.

Hint #1:   You observe or sense something—a clue to what you will eventually discover.

You discover nothing.

You react.

Hint #2:   You observe or sense something else (a different clue).

You discover nothing.

You react—a stronger reaction this time.

Hint #3:   You observe or sense something else (a different clue).

You make your discovery!

You react.

Get Ready to Write!

Think about your setting (*the autumn forest*), action (*walking in the woods*), and your discovery (*a wild turkey*). Begin with a sentence about strolling in the forest. Then, think about what kinds of sights, sounds, or feelings might hint (but not reveal) that a wild turkey is nearby. Each hint and each reaction should be stronger than the one before it. Follow the Magic of Three pattern to write a suspenseful paragraph!

Artful Connection   Make a gobbling turkey!

Who's Haunting This House?

Building suspense with the Magic of Three.

INTRODUCE

Introduce building suspense using the Magic of Three, reminding students to use sensory details to describe their hints.

MODEL

LITERATURE CONNECTION

The House that Drac Built
by Judy Sierra

In the Haunted House
by Eve Bunting

Demonstrate how the Magic of Three pattern works, using the example on page 53. Read the paragraph aloud and then ask students to pick out the three hints and reactions and to identify the revelation. Next, work through the activity on the *Who's Haunting This House?* student page (p. 65) as a whole-class activity.

Give students a lead sentence that sets a purpose for the action:

I carefully opened the door to the old abandoned house and peered inside.

Ask students to decide what they will discover. They will use that revelation to end their suspenseful paragraph. One class decided upon a goblin and used this sentence for their revelation:

A wild-eyed goblin jumped out from behind the closet door.

Ask students about what kinds of hints they might encounter for their chosen creature. Questions might include:

- If you were alone in this old abandoned house, what might you **HEAR** that would give you the feeling that something else might be in the house?
  a creaking of floorboards, the sound of glass breaking, a hideous laugh
- What might you **SEE** if something moved past you, just out of view?
  a large shadow, something brightly colored, something in the corner of your eye, a hand closing a door
- What might you **SENSE OR FEEL?**
  a feeling of being watched, a feeling that you are not alone, something touching your shoulder
- How would you **REACT** to each of these hints?
  nervous, heart pounding, you quicken your step, a shiver down your spine, hands tremble, knees feel weak, you begin to sweat, you gasp
- What **"RED FLAG"** words might you use to grab the reader's attention for each new hint?
  suddenly, all of a sudden, just then, the next thing I knew, before I knew it, in the blink of an eye

On chart paper, compose student responses into the Magic of Three pattern, thinking aloud as you do so. Your paragraph might look something like this:

I carefully opened the door to the old abandoned house and peered inside. Slowly, I stepped inside and closed the door behind me. My eyes were having difficulty focusing in the dimly lit hall. Suddenly, I heard the floorboards above me creaking. I stopped and listened. It was silent. There was nothing there. Just my imagination getting the best of me, I thought. I headed toward the stairs, anxious to go up and explore this rambling old wreck. As I reached the top of the stairs, a shadow raced across the floor. I quickly looked in the direction of the shadow, but it just seemed to disappear. I could feel my heart pounding in my chest as an icy chill ran through my body. Just then, a nearby door banged shut. I gasped and reached for the doorknob. As I opened the door, I was amazed to see a wild-eyed goblin staring straight at me!

ART CONNECTION

MATERIALS
- 18" x 24" manila construction paper, one piece for each student
- 18" x 24" black construction paper, one piece for each student
- scissors
- crayons, markers
- glue, tape
- X-acto™ knife (for teacher use)

PROCEDURE
1. Pass out the construction paper, and invite students to draw their own abandoned house. Encourage them to use as much of the paper as possible, so that they have a large house, and to include windows and doors. When they are finished, they can cut out the house.
2. As they are working, circulate around the room, and using the X-acto™ knife, cut out a window or door so that it can be opened.
3. Ask children to draw their "revelation" on a separate piece of paper. This is what they will place behind the door or window. They will need to be sure that their drawing will fit behind the window or door.
4. Now students mount their house on a large piece of black paper, being careful not to glue the cut window or door shut.
5. Students insert their revelation behind the flap.

GUIDED PRACTICE

When students have finished their abandoned house, distribute the student page and ask them to write a descriptive paragraph about the *who* or *what* hidden inside. Encourage them to use sensory details for their hints and the Magic of Three pattern for their structure. Remind them to use word referents to avoid giving away their revelation!

Presentation Idea

Invite students to read their suspense pieces aloud, using their house to reveal their discovery.

STUDENT SAMPLE

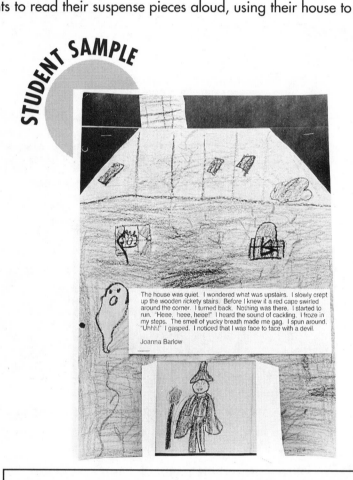

The house was quiet. I wondered what was upstairs. I slowly crept up the wooden rickety stairs. Before I knew it a red cape swirled around the corner. I turned back. Nothing was there. I started to run. "Heee, heee, heee!" I heard the sound of cackling. I froze in my steps. The smell of yucky breath made me gag. I spun around. "Uhhh!" I gasped. I noticed that I was face to face with a devil.

Joanna Barlow

The house was quiet. I wondered what was upstairs. I slowly crept up the wooden rickety stairs. Before I knew it, a red cape swirled around the corner. I turned back. Nothing was there. I started to run. "Heee, heee, heee!" I heard the sound of cackling. I froze in my steps. The smell of yucky breath made me gag. I spun around. "Uhhh!" I gasped. I noticed that I was face to face with a devil.

Name _____ Date _____

IMAGINE THAT . . .

▪▪▪

You are exploring an old abandoned house when suddenly you sense that you are not alone. Someone or something is in the house! You wonder what it is, but you discover nothing. You move on, and, for the second time, there is some hint—something you hear, see, or sense—that tells you something is near. Once again, nothing seems out of the ordinary, but you begin to feel nervous. You move cautiously on, and a third time you are made aware that you are not alone. You finally discover who or what it is haunting the house. You are surprised to see . . .

Artful Connection Make an abandoned house and hide what is haunting it behind a door or window—lift the flap and discover the revelation!

Writer's Technique Building suspense using the Magic of Three.

Here is the pattern that authors follow to create suspense using the Magic of Three:

Hint #1: You observe or sense something—a clue to what you will eventually discover

You discover nothing.

You react.

Hint #2: You observe or sense something else (a different clue).

You discover nothing

You react—a stronger reaction this time.

Hint #3: You observe or sense something else (a different clue).

You make your discovery!

You react.

Get Ready to Write!

Think about your setting (*the abandoned house*), action (*exploring*), and your discovery (*a _____*). Begin with a sentence about exploring an abandoned house. Then, think about what kinds of sights, sounds, or feelings might hint (but not reveal) that you are not alone. Each hint and each reaction should be stronger than the one before it. Follow the Magic of Three pattern to write a suspenseful paragraph!

Main Event

A successful short narrative story opens with an entertaining beginning that immediately draws the reader in. It is helpful to begin stories as close to the main event as possible—for example, if the story is about exploring a cave, begin at the mouth of the cave, not getting up the morning of the adventure, getting dressed, having breakfast, and planning the day. All of this extraneous detail tires the reader and shifts the focus away from the main event. Details about setting and character can be woven into the beginning action.

The opening should build up to a single, meaningful main event, which is, after all, the whole point of the story. The main event consists of the adventure, problem, or experience that changes the main character is some way.

Because of the importance of the main event, it should take up more space relative to other story elements; it will be longer than the beginning, than the description of the setting, than the solution, or the ending.

ELEMENTS OF A FULLY ELABORATED MAIN EVENT

Many times students rush through this all-important section by summarizing the main event with a very general sentence or two: *The bear chased me, but I got away.* How much more exciting this event would be if the author included:

1. a play-by-play account of the event *(the chase in slow motion)*

2. a detailed description of a story-critical setting, character, or object *(the bear)*

3. the main character's thoughts and feelings about the event *(how he or she felt during the chase)*

4. exclamations the story-critical character might make *(what would the main character say?)*

5. an explanation of how the event concludes *(how the main character escaped from the bear)*

Watch what happens to that summary when the author elaborates the main event with:

- slow-motion action
- description
- thoughts and feelings
- exclamations

Take a look at how these elements work in the following paragraph:

The bear was right behind me. I could feel his hot breath on the back of my neck. I pumped my arms and extended my stride, concentrating on getting beyond his grasp. I glanced over my shoulder to see what kind of lead I had. The large black bear looked right into my eyes, snarled, and bared his teeth. He struck out at me with his huge, razor-sharp claws. I took a deep a breath and screamed, "Leave me alone, you hairy beast!" as I dove into a nearby ditch. To my surprise, the bear ran right over me. My heart pounded as I cautiously lifted my head and peered around. No bear. I collapsed back into the ditch, breathing a sigh of relief. I was safe for the moment

An excellent exercise involves analyzing the paragraph above according to each element of main event: slow-motion action, description, thoughts and feelings, and exclamations. Write out the passage on chart paper or an overhead, and then have students help you color-code it, underlining each sentence in a different color to designate each main-event element.

KEEPING THE STORY FOCUSED ON THE MAIN EVENT

Another important tip to consider when working on main event: Most students' narrative pieces are actually short stories. Unlike a novel, made up of a series of events that escalate in intensity to a climactic main event, a short story really focuses on a single main event. Students who write stories that ramble (characterized by one event after another separated by "and then . . . and then . . . and then . . ."), and that depend upon all action and little else, are usually weak because the student has not focused on one significant event.

For example, a student writes about taking a ride on a magical flying bicycle. He flies over New York City, then over the Grand Canyon, then he flies to the moon, then he flies over the Alps, and then, and then, and then . . . The author has really created a grocery list of events that could be resequenced without affecting the story's outcome! A stronger story would involve choosing one of those events, say, flying over New York City, and retelling it with a balance of slow-motion action, description, thoughts and feelings, and exclamations.

So, how do students begin to transform summarized action into significant, meaningful, fully elaborated events? You can help them begin by asking and answering questions such as:

1. What did you do? (in slow motion!)

2. What did you observe? (using the five senses)

3. What did you think or feel?

4. What did you say?

The activities in this section are designed to help students focus on the main event and draw out the kind of elaboration that will turn summarized action into fully elaborated main events.

Leprechaun Chase

Creating a fully elaborated main event.

INTRODUCE

Introduce main event, reminding students that main events should be told through a balance of action, description, and dialogue.

LITERATURE CONNECTION

Leprechaun in My Basement
by Kathy Tucker

The Luckiest Leprechaun
by Justine Korman

Jack and the Leprechaun
by Ivan Robertson

MODEL

Model how you can use the questions on the *Leprechaun Chase* student page (p. 71) to generate ideas for your leprechaun chase. Think aloud about the exclamations you might make, how the action would look in slow motion, what thoughts and feelings you might have, and what observations you might make. Your charted notes might look like this:

EXCLAMATIONS
What in the world?
Feet, don't fail me now!
Look out!

OBSERVATIONS
wind whipping through hair
grass brushing against legs
scenery a blur

SLOW-MOTION ACTION
running as fast as I can
deep breath
pumped arms
chest heaving
got away—lost leprechaun
red in face
dropped to ground
leprechaun racing toward me with evil grin
huffed and puffed as chasing me
small feet a flurry of motion
disappeared behind the hill

THOUGHTS/FEELINGS
scared
focused on escaping
then relieved
exhausted from run

Once you've charted your ideas, with input from your students, think aloud for them as you turn the ideas into a complete paragraph, pointing out how you integrate all four elements of the main event. Your finished paragraph might look something like this:

There I was, running through the meadow with the leprechaun right behind me! "Feet, don't fail me now!" I shouted over my shoulder. I took a deep breath and concentrated on pounding my feet on the ground as fast as I could. I pumped hard with my arms to help me gain speed. The leprechaun was huffing and puffing wildly, his small feet a flurry of motion. Everything around me passed by in a blur, the wind whipping through my hair. I felt the grass brush against my legs as I ran. Finally, I got away! I was relieved and exhausted, red in the face, my chest heaving a huge sigh of relief!

The key is to stretch out the moment, extending each summarized action (*I ran*) into smaller parts (*I took a deep breath and concentrated on pounding my feet on the ground as fast as I could. I pumped hard with my arms to help me gain speed*). Notice the sentence variety. It is not just a list of *and then . . . and then . . . and then . . .*

ART CONNECTION

MATERIALS
- oaktag
- markers
- tape
- an unsharpened pencil for each student

PREPARATION
Cut out two 4" x 6" oaktag sheets for each student.

PROCEDURE
1. Distribute two 4"x 6" oaktag sheets to each student.

2. Invite students to draw a running leprechaun on one sheet and a picture of themselves running on the other. Pictures must be large and should be colored in bold colors. (It is helpful to have books or pictures of leprechauns on hand so that students have some idea what a leprechaun looks like.) Students may add a simple, lightly colored background to each picture—ground and sky.

3. As students finish their drawings, circulate with a roll of tape. Tape pictures securely, back to back, to the pencil as pictured.

4. Show students how to hold the pencil spinner between their palms and rub their palms back and forth together, which causes the picture to spin, creating the optical illusion of a chase!

GUIDED PRACTICE

When students have completed their spinners, invite them to describe the chase in slow motion, using the prompts from the student page. To help students focus on the main event and include a balance of action, description, and dialogue, you might ask them, "What might you do, moment by moment, during the chase?" "What would you see, hear, and feel?" "What might you say as you ran from the leprechaun?"

STUDENT SAMPLE

There I was running through the meadow with the leprechaun right behind me! I ran faster than I ever had before! I could feel sweat forming on my forehead. My heart was pounding extremely fast. I wanted to stop but then the leprechaun would catch me. I was very determined to get away. I yelled, "Help! I'm getting chased by a leprechaun!" Even if someone did hear me, they probably wouldn't believe me. I ran harder and faster. I tried to catch my breath. The leprechaun was fast also. I didn't want to look back because I was worried that it would slow me down. I could tell he was gaining on me though! The trees looked like a big blur as I sped past them. My feet were barely touching the ground. I could feel the wind rushing through my hair. As I ran the dry air made my throat sting. "What would happen to me if he caught me?" I thought to myself. I was really worried. I zig-zagged through the tall giant like pines. The

leprechaun was getting confused while watching me. He got so dazed, that he fell down! When I heard the resounding THUMP, I stopped and turned to look down at him. His eyes were swirling around and around. His tall green tophat fell off of his big round head which was the size of a beach ball. I felt so relieved. I finally got away, and I wanted to go home and have dinner.

Leprechaun Chase Student Page

Name _____ Date _____

One magical spring day, you get chased across a meadow by a leprechaun! In the end, you get away!

Writer's Technique   Writing a fully elaborated main event.

Artful Connection   Make a leprechaun spinner, which creates the optical illusion of a speedy race between you and the leprechaun.

Get Ready to Write!   After you've finished your leprechaun spinner and have used it to illustrate the big chase, think about what it would be like to be chased by a leprechaun. Think about the chase in slow motion, moment by moment. Put yourself in the situation and think about these questions.

What did you exclaim as you ran?

_____

What did you do? (in slow motion, one movement at a time!)

_____

What did the leprechaun do? (in slow motion, one movement at a time!)

_____

What did you notice as you ran? (Use the five senses.)

_____

How were you feeling?

_____

On another piece of paper, brainstorm answers to each question. Then turn your answers into complete sentences that describe a fully elaborated main event. Begin with this sentence if you like:

There I was, running through the meadow with the leprechaun right behind me!

Magic Carpet Ride

 **Creating a fully elaborated main event.**

INTRODUCE

LITERATURE CONNECTION

Introduce main event, reminding students to focus on one event and to use a balance of action, description, and dialogue.

Tuesday by David Wiesner

MODEL

Model how the questions on the *Magic Carpet Ride* student page (p. 75) can be used to generate ideas for your magic carpet ride. Think aloud about the exclamations you might make, how the action would look in slow motion, what thoughts and feelings you might have, and what observations you might make. Encourage students to chime in and add their own ideas. Your charted notes might look like this:

EXCLAMATION
Wow!
Yikes!
Whoa, there . . .

OBSERVATIONS
tiny city, far below
cars and trucks like ants
no people
wind whipping across face
puffy clouds drifting by
birds flying by

SLOW MOTION
soaring high over city
grasping edges of carpet
holding on for dear life
carpet swoops and dips
takes a nosedive and plunges to ground
    but slows and lands safely

THOUGHTS/FEELINGS
amazed
scared
shocked
relieved

Then craft your ideas into a complete paragraph, thinking aloud about your choices as you do so. Your paragraph might look something like this:

I could hardly believe I was soaring over the city on a magic carpet. "Wow!" I yelled as I grasped the edges of the carpet and held on for dear life. The carpet swooped and dipped like a graceful bird. I felt the air whip across my face and stared at the puffy clouds nearby. A flock of birds flew by, squawking in surprise at the sight of me zooming past. I looked down and gasped at the sight of the buildings and cars and trucks, all the size of ants. Suddenly, the carpet took a nosedive, and I shrieked. My mouth fell open in shock as we plunged toward the ground. Just in the nick of time, the carpet slowed and landed safely. My wild ride was over!

To make this work, remind students to stretch out the moment, extending summarized action (*I flew*) into smaller parts (*I grasped the edges of the carpet and held on for dear life*) and incorporating dialogue and feelings.

ART CONNECTION

MATERIALS

- construction paper in assorted colors
- scissors
- a variety of yarn and ribbon
- tape

PREPARATION

Prepare enough "magic carpets" for each student. For each carpet:

Fold a piece of 8½" x 11" construction paper in half, as shown in Step 1.

With the paper folded, cut horizontal slits in the paper, from the folded edge to about one inch from the opposite edge. (See Step 2.)

Cut enough 8½" x ½" to 8½" x 1" construction paper strips for weaving. Also cut a variety of 8½" lengths of yarn and ribbon (widths will vary).

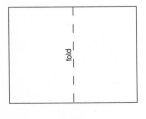

fold

Step 1

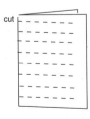

cut

Step 2

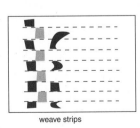

weave strips

Step 3

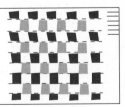
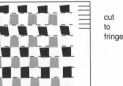

cut to fringe

Step 4

PROCEDURE

1. Distribute slit paper to students along with colored strips and yarn and ribbon.

2. Demonstrate how to weave in alternate over-under pattern, running 8 ½" strips between the larger slit pieces, as shown in Step 3 on page 73.

3. Show students how to slide woven strips close together so their edges touch.

4. As students complete their weaving, use tape to secure strips to the back side of carpet.

5. Show students how to fringe the edges of their carpet by cutting narrow slits into both short ends of the paper, as shown in Step 4.

6. Optional: Have students draw themselves in a seated position (to scale with their carpets) and staple the figures to their carpets!

GUIDED PRACTICE

Once students have created their magic carpet, remind them to choose a single destination or problem for their ride and to describe the action in slow motion. Invite them to use the questions on the student page and remind them not to simply string together a "grocery list" of actions.

Display Idea

Back a bulletin board with sky-blue paper and add some puffy white clouds. Staple carpets 3-D style to board along with main events.

STUDENT SAMPLE

I could hardly believe I was soaring over the city on a magic carpet. "Weee!!" I yelled. I gently raked my side to side to steer my direction. My heart felt light as a piece of buttered popcorn. I felt free, like I had been locked up for many years. Also I felt relaxed. So relaxed I laid down and closed my eyes. The carpet was smooth and silkey which made my arms cool in the hot weather. How the carpet moved is hard to explain. It rocked me side to side like a rocking chair, slow and steady. It also went up and down. Waves in the carpet flowed lightly and gently. So air was rushing all around me. I opened my eyes and noticed all the tiny people. They reminded me of ants by there size and by how they moved. Always busy. Like the city was a giant chocolate chip cookie and everyone wanted some of it. The buildings were like giants peering up at me. I also noticed the birds. I never known how in control they are with flying. There big, beautiful, graceful wings seemed to do it themselves. I heard them singing

and some smelled like the ocean. I broke in to a smile that was bigger than all of the buildings put together. I closed my eyes again. "Huhh," I sighed. I was very contented. After a minute or two I opened my eyes. Then I saw my fate. I was heading straight for the Empire State ready to crash! It was to late to turn. I would have to think up some other way, if I could!

Magic Carpet Ride Student Page

Name _____ Date _____

IMAGINE THAT . . .

You are taking a magic carpet ride over a big city.

Writer's Technique   Creating a fully elaborated main event.

Artful Connection   Weave your own magic carpet of paper, yarn, and ribbon!

Get Ready to Write!   Imagine soaring on your magic carpet. Think about your ride in slow motion, moment by moment. Put yourself in the situation and answer these questions.

What did you exclaim as you soared through the sky?

_____

What did you do? (in slow motion, one movement at a time!)

_____

_____

_____

How did the carpet move? (in slow motion, one movement at a time!)

_____

What did you notice as you flew? (Use the five senses.)

_____

_____

_____

How were you feeling?

_____

Now turn your answers into complete sentences, and put them together in an action-packed paragraph. Begin with this sentence if you like:

I could hardly believe I was soaring over the city on a magic carpet.

Ouch!

 **Creating a fully elaborated main event.**

INTRODUCE

LITERATURE CONNECTION

5 Little Monkeys Jumping on the Bed
by Eileen Christelow

To start this activity, ask students to think back to a time when something uncomfortable happened to them. You might want to describe your own experience, pointing out how that particular event seemed to stretch out forever. Discuss how writers can stretch out time by using slow-motion action, description, and dialogue, and how these techniques make for a fully elaborated main event.

MODEL

Model how the questions on the *Ouch!* student page (p. 79) can be used to generate ideas for describing how you trip and fall. Think aloud about the exclamations you might make, how the fall would look in slow motion, what thoughts and feelings you might have as you take your tumble, and what observations you might make on your way down. Encourage students to contribute their own ideas. Your charted notes might look like this:

EXCLAMATION
Ouch!
Holy cow!
Yikes!
Youch!
I need a Band-Aid™!

OBSERVATIONS
beautiful day
scene blurred as fell down

SLOW MOTION
strolling along
tripped
shoes slipped on gravel
feet skidded
hands waved wildly
heart pounded
threw hand out in front to break fall
hit pavement knees-first
started crying
whimpered for help
rubbed sore knee

THOUGHTS/FEELINGS
panicky
visions of casts and bandages
intense pain
throbbing knee

Select items from the chart and create a paragraph, thinking aloud about your choices. The paragraph might look like this:

There I was, happily strolling along, when all of a sudden I felt myself trip! My shoes slipped on the gravel, and my feet skidded this way and that. "Holy cow!" I yelled as I waved my hands wildly in the air! My heart began to pound, and I threw my hands in front of me, trying to break my fall. Visions of casts and bandages flashed across my mind. POW! I hit the pavement, knees first. "Youch!" I cried. My lips began to quiver, and my eyes filled with tears. My knee throbbed. "Get me a Band-Aid!™" I whimpered as I rubbed my aching knee.

The key is to stretch out the moment, extending each summarized action (*I fell*) into smaller parts. (*My shoes slipped on the gravel, and my feet skidded this way and that. "Holy cow!" I yelled as I waved my hands wildly in the air! My heart began to pound, and I threw my hands in front of me, trying to break my fall.*) Notice how dialogue and the narrator's feelings are woven in.

ART CONNECTION

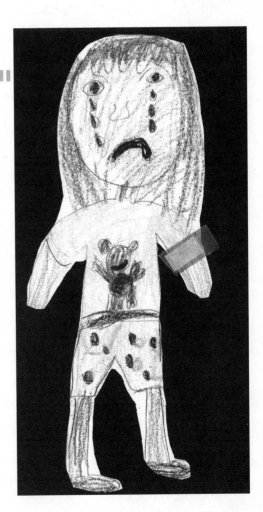

MATERIALS
- construction paper, preferably 8½" x 14" or larger
- crayons
- markers
- Band-Aids™

PROCEDURE
1. Have students draw a full-length self-portrait on a piece of large construction paper held the long way. Encourage them to draw a large figure that will fill the whole page. They should be sure to incorporate a facial expression that shows how they are feeling after the fall. Color in brightly.

2. Add a Band-Aid™ to the "injured" body part.

GUIDED PRACTICE

The art component can be completed before or after students write about their fall. Pass out the student page and encourage students to plan their paragraph by answering the questions on it. Then ask them to construct a paragraph describing their fall in slow motion.

Display Idea
Create a playground safety bulletin board or bind the pictures and paragraphs into a class book titled OUCH!

STUDENT SAMPLE

I was walking through the pool. Squeak! Plm! I tripped over a rubber ducky. I felt my body fall foward and my legs flung backward. "Ahhhhh'hhh." I yelled as I saw the pool floor get closer

Before:
I tripped and fell. I cut my

arm

and closer. Boom! Bang. I fell to the ground with a thud. I hugged the boo boo on my arm. I decided never to daydream as I am walking in a pool again.

Joanna April 4, 1999

Ouch! Student Page

Name _____ Date _____

IMAGINE THAT . . .

You stumble, trip, and fall down....Ouch!

Writer's Technique   Creating a fully elaborated main event.

Artful Connection   Create a self-portrait and add a Band-Aid™ to cover the "ouch"!

Get Ready to Write!   Imagine you trip and fall. (That's the summary!) Think about your fall in slow motion. Put yourself in the situation and answer these questions.

What did you exclaim as you fell?

_____

What did you do to try to block your fall? (in slow motion, one movement at a time!)

_____

_____

What were you thinking or worrying about as you fell?

_____

_____

What did you notice as you fell? (Use the five senses.)

_____

_____

_____

_____

How were you feeling?

_____

_____

Write your answers in complete sentences to make a fully elaborated main event. Begin with this sentence if you like:

There I was, happily strolling along, when all of a sudden I felt myself trip!

79

Resources

Anderson, Hans Christian. *The Little Mermaid*. New York: Dover, 1995.

Brett, Jan. *The Gingerbread Baby*. New York: Putnam, 1999.

—. *The Mitten*. New York: Putnam, 1989.

Briggs, Raymond. *The Snowman*. New York: Random House, 1999.

Bunting, Eve. *In the Haunted House*. Boston: Houghton Mifflin, 1994.

—. *A Turkey for Thanksgiving*. Boston: Houghton Mifflin, 1995.

Carle, Eric. *Does a Kangaroo Have a Mother?* New York: HarperCollins, 2000.

—. *The Grouchy Ladybug*. New York: Harperfestival, 1999.

—. *The Very Busy Spider*. New York: Philomel Books, 1995.

Cherry, Lynne. *The Great Kapok Tree*. Orlando: Harcourt, 2000.

Christelow, Eileen. *5 Little Monkeys Jumping on the Bed*. New York: Clarion, 1986.

Climo, Shirley. *Egyptian Cinderella*. New York: Harper Collins, 1991.

—. *Irish Cinderlad* New York: HarperCollins, 1997.

Cummings, Pat. *Clean Your Room, Harvey Moon!* New York: Simon & Schuster, 1994.

Dahl, Roald. *The BFG*. New York: Penguin, 1998.

Ehlert, Lois. *Snowballs*. Orlando: Harcourt , 1999.

Fowler, Allan. *How Do You Know It's Fall?* New York: Children's Press, 1992.

—. *Turkeys that Fly and Turkeys That Don't*. New York: Children's Press, 1997.

Fox, Mem. *Tough Boris*. Orlando: Harcourt, 1998.

Galdone, Paul. *The Gingerbread Boy*. Boston: Houghton Mifflin, 1993.

George, Jeanne Craighead. *Dear Rebecca, Winter Is Here*. New York: HarperCollins, 1995.

Gibbons, Gail. *Pirates*. Boston: Little Brown, 1999.

Gwynne, Fred. *The King Who Rained*. New York: Simon and Schuster, 1975.

Hess, Paul. *Rainforest Animals*. Zero to Ten, 1998.

Hickox, Rebecca. *The Golden Sandal: A Middle Eastern Cinderella*. Holiday House, 1998.

Isadora, Rachel. *The Little Mermaid*. New York: Putnam, 1998.

Keats, Ezra Jack. *Snowy Day*. New York: Penguin, 1976.

Kellogg, Steven. *Jack and the Beanstalk*. New York: Morrow Publications, 1997.

Korman, Justine. *The Luckiest Leprechaun*. Bridgewater Books, 2000.

Lionni, Leo. *Frederick*. New York: Knopf, 1987.

Littlewood, Valerie. *Scarecrow!* New York: Penguin, 1995.

Maestro, Besty. *Snow Day*. New York: Scholastic , 1989.

Martin Jr., Bill. *Barn Dance*. New York: Holt, 1991.

McNaughton, Colin. *Captain Abdul's Pirate School*. Candlewick, 1996.

—. *Suddenly*. Orlando: Harcourt Brace, 1998.

Osborne, Mary Pope. *Mermaid Tales*. New York: Scholastic, 1999.

Pratt, Kristin Joy. *A Walk in the Rainforest*. Dawn Publications, 1992.

Robbins, Ken. *Autumn Leaves*. New York: Scholastic, 1998.

Robertson, Ivan. *Jack and the Leprechaun*. New York: Random House, 2000.

Rogasky, Barbara. *Winter Poems*. New York: Scholastic, 1994.

San Souci, Robert D. *Feathertop*. Bantam Doubleday Dell, 1995.

—. *Sukey and the Mermaid*. New York: Simon & Schuster, 1996.

Schnur, Steven. *Autumn, an Alphabet Acrostic*. Boston: Houghton Mifflin, 1997.

Scieszka, Jon. *Not-So-Jolly Roger*. New York: Penguin, 1993.

Sierra, Judy. *The House that Drac Built*. Orlando: Harcourt Brace , 1998.

Steig, William. *Brave Irene*. New York: Farrar, Straus and Giroux, 1998

Strickland, Brad. *Jack and the Beanstalk*. Lyrick Publications, 1976.

Thaler, Mike. *Cinderella Bigfoot*. New York: Cartwheel Books, 1997.

Titherington, Jeanne. *A Place for Ben*. New York: Wm. Morrow & Co., 1999.

Tucker, Kathy. *The Leprechaun in the Basement*. Whitman & Co., 1999.

Wiesner, David. *Tuesday*. New York: Clarion, 1991.

Woods, Audrey. *King Bidgood's in the Bathtub*. Orlando: Harcourt, 1985.

Yolen, Jane. *Owl Moon*. New York: Putnam, 1987.